Decorate
to speculate

Decorate to speculate

52 brilliant ideas to increase your house value

Giles Kime

CAREFUL NOW

Just in case you're the litigious kind we thought we ought to point out a few things. Like all the great small print says – the value of your investment may go up as well as down. The ideas in here should enable you to make the most of your home as an investment but we can't be responsible for how you use this information. Do be careful, get architects and builders to help on the really big jobs, make sure you get all the appropriate planning permission, don't wear your brand new designer jeans when painting and always put the lid back on the polyfilla.

Copyright © The Infinite Ideas Company Limited, 2008

The right of Giles Kime to be identified as the author of this book has been asserted in accordance with the Copyright, Designs and Patents Act 1988

First published in 2008 by
The Infinite Ideas Company Limited
36 St Giles
Oxford, OX1 3LD
United Kingdom
www.infideas.com

A CIP catalogue record for this book is available from the British Library

ISBN 978-1-905940-39-4

Brand and product names are trademarks or registered trademarks of their respective owners.

Designed by Baseline Arts Ltd, Oxford
Typeset by Sparks, Oxford
Printed in China

Brilliant ideas

Brilliant features

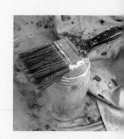

Each chapter of this book is designed to provide you with an inspirational idea that you can read quickly and put into practice straight away.

Throughout you'll find three features that will help you get right to the heart of the idea:

■ *Here's an idea for you ...* Take it on board and give it a go – right here, right now. Get an idea of how well you're doing so far.

■ *Defining idea ...* Words of wisdom from masters and mistresses of the art, plus some interesting hangers-on.

■ *How did it go?* If at first you do succeed, try to hide your amazement. If, on the other hand, you don't, then this is where you'll find a Q and A that highlights common problems and how to get over them.

Introduction

Learn the art of creating a home that is also a profitable investment and you'll wonder why you never did it before.

Decorate to Speculate is for people who see their homes as more than just a place to live. It's for those of you who appreciate the fact that buying a property is the single biggest investment in your life which, unlike your car or your next holiday (and in some cases your pension scheme), will appreciate in value rather than plummet the minute that you sign the cheque. It's tax efficient, too. Unlike so many other types of investment you won't pay anything in tax if a property is your primary residence. For every £1000 you earn from working, well over a third (sometimes more) will disappear in tax and national insurance. When the value of your home increases by the same amount you get to keep every penny.

But, like any investment, it needs careful handling. In the same way that a work of art will only rise in value if everyone wants it, a property will only appreciate if it has a 'wow' factor that sets it apart from the competition. The result is that you have to treat your home not as an expression of your own tastes but as a development that will have the maximum possible appeal to the target market that you have identified.

It sounds ruthless doesn't it? And, frankly, who wants to live in a development anyway? Well, partly that depends on the nature of the development. The chances are that if a property is designed so that it appeals to a wide audience, then you'll probably like it too. And if you don't, then you can always console yourself with the fact that at least you're making money out of it.

Remember, too, that when you make choices about a property, there are literally hundreds of routes that you can follow. Choosing a route that will enhance a property should be no great hardship. The secret of decorating to speculate is simply to create a property that everyone will like, not just you. And whilst these choices necessarily involve money, bear in mind that you can spend a fortune on luxury kitchens, bathrooms and fancy furnishings and not add as much value as you could with a refurbishment project costing half the price. The more skilled you become as a developer, the more you'll learn how to identify those elements in a property that are worth investing in.

But there's no doubt that creating and living in a development requires a huge amount of discipline, research and a certain mindset. And there are all sorts of tricks that will help, too, such as paring down the contents of a room so that it looks its chic best. This book will demonstrate that a good development is not just about adding as much space as you can, willy-nilly. It's more subtle than that; sometimes it's about creating an environment with interior schemes that are suggestive of a lifestyle that potential buyers aspire to. For many of them these are schemes that they would find almost impossible to create themselves, so they'll effectively be paying you to do it for them.

The process starts even before you are in a property. And the art of development isn't just about making the right changes – it's also about finding a property to which you can add value. As you view a place, you need to look for achievable ways to improve it beyond recognition. And we're not just talking about upmarket properties here; the principles are exactly the same at every level of the market. You'll achieve the same percentage gains on a modestly priced property as you do on a high value one. And the property that you own might not just be your own home. In periods of low interest rates it is tempting to buy other properties to let out, or to hang on to a property when you move on, renting it out until you decide to sell.

The joy of decorating to speculate is that it is a skill that will improve every time you refurbish. What seems like an awesome undertaking when you buy your first property, will seem like child's play when you are into your third. But this book isn't just for people who want to 'turn over' properties as soon as the paint has dried. It is also for people who are taking a long term view but want to ensure that any decisions that they make are the right ones. In that sense, it's really for everyone who owns a home.

1

A few home truths

Whichever way you look at it, money spent on your home is one of the best investments you'll ever make.

It's easy to overlook, but simply having the right mindset is a crucial ingredient.

Pension fund managers might beg to differ (although let's face it, they're hardly likely to be the most objective people on the subject) but one of the most copper-bottomed investments you'll ever make is in bricks and mortar. Look at any ten-year period in recent history and you'll see prices steadily rising, sometimes quickly, sometimes slowly – and sometimes with some turbulence in between. Every ten-year period that includes even the most precipitous drops will include peaks which more than compensate.

'But, but, but…' wail the pension advisers 'investing money in your home is no substitute for long term investment in a pension scheme.' And on the whole they're right; even allowing for the vast fees involved, the tax advantages of pensions – and their long term growth – means that they are an essential part of any sound financial planning. But, so too is shrewd investment in property that won't just provide you with a roof but also with financial security in years to come. It would be equally as risky to invest all your expendable income in a pension and little, if nothing, in your home.

Unless you're lucky, clever or a bit of both, buying and investing in your own home is rarely a guarantee of overnight returns. But if you are going to invest money in putting a roof over your head you might as well protect your investment. In the long term, shrewd enhancement of a property can offer extremely healthy returns on the time, money and thought that you plough into a property.

The bottom might fall out of the market, or interest rates spiral upwards, but the joy of taking a long term view is that you'll always have long enough to make up any losses. The secret is never to expose yourself to too much debt; always calculate how much your payments would be if interest rates rose by fifty or hundred per cent just to give yourself a reality check. Also, if possible, try to keep reserves of cash on deposit, so that if interest rates rise, you'll get an increase in income to offset higher costs.

When you're looking for a property, it doesn't necessarily mean that you need to buy a home in an area that will show an exponential rise in value. First and foremost, this is your home that we're talking about, not some buy-to-let investment in some dodgy part of town. Remember that you've got to live there too, and you don't have to buy a house between an abattoir and a high security prison just to get a good return on your money. There are also gains to be had in areas that have already seen significant price rises.

The secret lies simply in looking for properties to which you can add value. Could you convert the loft into another bedroom? Would the scrappy front garden be better used as off street parking? Could the warren of tiny rooms be turned into a free flowing, open plan space? Collectively, a number of even quite minor changes can achieve a whole that is far greater than a sum of its parts.

And the investment needn't be huge. You'd be surprised, too, at how much even the most minor work can completely transform a house; while many prospective buyers find it hard to see grubby paintwork and tired old carpets, they can be equally be blown away by crisp fresh colours and a stripped floor.

Remember that there is a breed of buyer who isn't just buying bricks and mortar when they are buying a property – they're also buying your time. Some people, for example, a hard-working couple who can't spare the man-hours or the inconvenience involved in even the most basic refurbishment are likely to pay over the odds for a home in which they can simply unpack rather than start flicking through the *Yellow Pages*.

However, what is most crucial is that you don't just enhance but also protect your investment. Because the sums involved are so large, many people become quite devil-may-care when it comes to the value of their property. Yet, unlike a pension scheme, it is the one area of our finances over which you have the most control – exercise it.

Here's an idea for you...

If you need proof of the fact that property offers a solid investment, do some research into how the prices of local properties have risen. There are plenty of sources to look at ... good places to look are the land registry and back issues of local newspapers.

Defining idea...

'The best investment on earth is earth.'
LOUIS J GLICKMAN

How did it go?

Q **Won't treating my home as an investment mean upheaval?**

A *Maximising the value of your home doesn't necessarily involve buying and selling on a regular basis. Of course, the more you move, the quicker you'll realise the gain – but alternatively you may prefer to take a long term view.*

Q **But if I opt for the 'high churn' approach of moving home regularly, won't it involve a lots of costs such as stamp duty, legal fees and agents' commission?**

A *Yes, it will. But in a rising market there should still be a sufficient margin, particularly if you are selling high and buying low.*

Q **But don't you pay tax on the profit, too?**

A *Not if it is your primary residence. This is one of the reasons that property investment is so lucrative. When you have a salaried job, it attracts income tax – when you buy and sell houses all the profit is yours.*

2

Take the holistic approach to your home

A house or apartment consists of integral parts that all impact on one another – and all need to be treated with equal care.

So before you rush straight in, consider the property as a whole.

Every investment plan needs a strategy – and like all the best strategic planning, yours should start with a look at the bigger picture rather than the minutiae. A building is like a machine that consists of different components that all impact on one another, so it's important to establish how best that machine can be tuned – or perhaps completely re-configured.

Start this process with a 'space audit' of your home, which involves treating it as though it is a new build on the architect's drawing board. And like an architect, it's worth doing two things – drawing a scale plan of each floor and working out the total amount of floor space in each room. Any building, whatever its style or period, comprises a surprising amount of flexible space that can easily be tailored to your needs. In addition, you'll also discover plenty of unexploited areas: in a roof space, on landings, under stairs – even outside – that can all be put to good use.

Rather than simply writing the amount of floor area on the plan, work out the percentage of your living space that is devoted to certain activities such as eating, cooking, sleeping, relaxing or working. While you may not necessarily act on the figures you create, the analysis will help you focus on whether space is being well used.

For example, if you spend a great deal of time in your kitchen and the latter is just 20% of your living space and your living and dining space is 40% you might decide to look at ways that you could create a balance that better suits your needs. One possible solution would be to simply extend the kitchen. Alternatively, you may decide to create a kitchen/dining room in the space currently devoted to the living room and dining room and use the area occupied by the kitchen as smaller living room. When looking at storage you may find that while 15% of your space is devoted to spare rooms, only 5% is devoted to storage, so you might decide to use a spare room as a dedicated dressing room, complete with fitted cupboards.

Here's an idea for you... **As well as calculating the floor area of your own home, take the same approach to a property that you may be thinking of buying. And as well as comparing the total floor areas, compare the floor areas of individual rooms. Also remember to take into account the fact that the overall figures provided may include garages and outhouses.**

The important part of this process is that it will help you to be dispassionate about planning the way that you use the space in your home. Too often we are wedded to the original layout of a property – and the way the space is allocated – when often it would have simply evolved over time, with very little thought or planning. And, however disruptive it might seem, removing or adding a wall tends to be quite a straightforward business.

But it's not just about you, is it? Before acting on any of these calculations, consider whether the layout caters purely for your own tastes and needs, or whether it would be attractive to a potential buyer. You may decide that you are prepared to sacrifice a bedroom in order to create a large hotel-style bathroom – but if it's at the expense of a spare room or home office you may be creating a layout that doesn't suit everyone's tastes or needs. When planning a layout it is essential to remember that balance is all.

Once you understand the concept of balancing the different types of living area in your home, you'll want to work out the relative proportions for the various com- plementary spaces. This is one of reasons that, however good your calculations and planning are, it is helpful if you live in a property before you make any long term decisions. Not only will you get a feel for which rooms suit which purposes, but also which are too big and which are too small.

'*Nothing is as dangerous in architecture as dealing with separated problems.*'

ALVAR AALTO

Defining idea...

How did it go?

Q **But what if I am building an extension – how do I get an idea of the perfect size for a living room or kitchen?**

A *Research is all. Try to get a handle on how big existing rooms are and also those of others properties that you spend time in. The scale plans that estate agents produce are an ideal way to learn about the ideal amount of space for a room. When you look around a house that is on the market never look at a room without referring to the plan to ascertain what the dimensions are. The more you do this, the more you will enhance your sense of how big a room should be.*

Q **I realise that storage is important but is it really worth sacrificing a bedroom or large bathroom for a dressing room?**

A *It really depends on the size of the property and the number of people that it will accomodate. Remember that good storage will have a significant impact on the rest of the property.*

Q **Can a dressing room serve any other functions?**

A *Yes. The trick with a dressing room is to combine some other function such as a spare room or home office. Even with a pair of large fitted cupboards and a chest of drawers there should be room for a bed or desk.*

3

En suite dreams

Arranging a bedroom and bathroom in a self contained hotel-style configuration can't fail to seduce potential buyers.

It is, after all, an area to rest, relax and pamper ourselves!

Estate agents used to have just one thing on their minds when it came to selling houses – an all-singing, all-dancing kitchen. And, while that is still very much the case, there is another room that they believe plays a key role as a buyer magnet – an all-singing, all-dancing, hotel-style bathroom.

So, what has changed? Well, it isn't a new obsessive interest in hygiene. Instead, many of us are travelling more. And at the same time hotels – even relatively modest establishments – are paying much more attention to their bathrooms with the result that they tend to be bigger and more luxuriously fitted out than ever before.

But there is also one feature of a hotel bathroom that we've grown to love – namely, that it is seamlessly joined to the bedroom. Even in our own homes there is something wonderfully luxurious about being cocooned in your own space. The result is that there is now more and more reason to reconfigure the layout of a house, so that the main bedroom has an en suite.

The problem lies in doing so without compromising either the overall arrangement of the rooms – or the bedroom itself. In many cases, creating an en suite is a relatively straightforward process that can be as simple as removing a wall between a bedroom and a neighbouring bathroom. But, even in this situation, pay attention to how moving the door might impact on the layout in the rest of the room.

The joy of this kind of project is that while it can cause huge amounts of upheaval, removing a wall between two rooms is relatively inexpensive – and, done well, the advantages are disproportionate to the investment required. When potential buyers see a beautifully designed en suite bathroom, they don't just think of the financial investment that you have made, they think of all the inconvenience that they will be saved.

Here's an idea for you... **When planning an en suite bathroom create a scale drawing of your bedroom and bathroom space and cut out shapes that represent different elements – the bed, storage, bath, towel rail, sink, etc. It will help you to decide how best to arrange the space and where to place the adjoining door.**

There is no doubt that bedrooms can be difficult rooms to plan; by the time you've accommodated a bed, storage plus radiators and allowed for the fact that neither of these can face a window, you aren't left with a great deal of room for moving the position of the door to the en suite. Even if you choose to banish storage to another room (always a good plan) and go to the expense of fitting underfloor heating (ditto) you are still left with a design challenge.

A more costly option is if the main bedroom is nowhere near a bathroom. In this case, you'll have to move the bathroom next door and the chances are that it won't be a room you especially want to sacrifice – or it won't necessarily be one that lends itself to conversion to a bathroom. The only solution will be to consider moving the main bedroom. If the neighbouring room is very large, it might be worth considering a room that combines both a bathroom and a dressing room which will help to make the most of the space – the layout could either be open plan, or you could divide the space into both a bathroom and a dressing room.

In a typical terraced house, the ideal location for an en suite bathroom and bedroom is sufficiently removed from the main hub of the house such as in a roof extension, that offers the most flexible space – and won't mean sacrificing a room.

If the main bedroom is large, you may be tempted to carve up the space by fitting a partition wall. In a beautiful period house, this can be a mistake as you are trading a room with great proportions for two that don't have any. In this instance, a good solution is to create a bathroom 'zone' divided by a low freestanding wall that hides the plumbing and the bath – but which also allows easy access around either end. The bathing 'zone' can be distinguished from the rest of the room by a different type of flooring.

For guest rooms there is a space-efficient alternative to the all-singing-all-dancing en suite: an adjoining room with a shower, WC and wash basins offers all the privacy and convenience of a large scale en suite but occupies a space that is a fraction of the size.

'Solitude is painful when one is young but delightful when one is in maturity.'
ALBERT EINSTEIN

Defining idea...

How did it go?

Q **Our bathroom is currently bang next door to our bedroom but they aren't interconnected. Is there really any point in going to the effort of joining the two?**

A *Much depends on the property. In a small flat the advantage would be less than in a high value five bedroom house. For families they are the perfect way to create privacy for parents – or for guests.*

Q **And what about properties where there is just one bedroom?**

A *In this case, it may not make much sense to create an en suite bathroom. However, if there isn't room for a full scale en suite, you could consider creating a small shower room that adjoins a bedroom.*

Q **But is there any point if I live alone?**

A *Remember that decorating to speculate is not just about you – it's about the person who may potentially buy your home.*

Q **Can a property have too many bathrooms?**

A *Not really. As long as they fit comfortably into the available space – and don't compromise any other facilities – then you could fit as many as you like.*

4

Hot looks for houses

We tend to have but a fleeting relationship with the front of our properties, but houses – like people – are often judged on first appearances.

It's time then to reveal the secret to creating great kerb appeal.

When leaving or returning home we are usually too preoccupied with some other activity – parking a car, carrying shopping, herding children, looking for elusive keys – to look too closely at the façade of a house, the doorway, the windows, the path. Yet these are exactly the elements that will be under scrutiny when a prospective buyer comes to inspect a house – and, if anything, because they are the first things on view they will be magnified with disproportionate intensity.

The outside of a house frequently incorporates a diverse range of different elements – from iron work and door furniture to paving and lighting – so it should be treated like a scheme inside the house, where possible it should combine a harmonious palette of colours. Try to keep colours and textures complementary – from the paving to the shrubs that you choose.

The best way to see what works – and what doesn't – is to look at other houses. A walk around a neighbourhood will throw up plenty of ideas for what you might like to achieve on your own home. But rather than simply imitating what you see on

Here's an idea for you... **Rather than spending hours staring at the front of your house, take a photograph of it. Studying a photograph often makes you much more objective – and makes it much easier to compare with the façades of other houses.**

other houses let your imagination run freely. A well put together scheme is a cost effective way to make yours stand out from the crowd. Most important is an appearance that gives the impression or a well loved and cared for house.

You may notice that those buildings that don't reveal much about their interiors trend often look smarter and more intriguing than those that do. Plantation shutters, etched glass or sheer panels can all help to present a sleek face to the world.

CREATING A SLEEK, CONTEMPORARY FEEL

While the look you create should be broadly in keeping with the architecture of the house there are plenty of ways that you can project a sharp, modern feel. The clean lines of slate are ideal for this purpose – as is door furniture and lighting in a sleek, minimal style and a highly reflective finish. When choosing paint, matt black and greys are the perfect option for woodwork and, in glazed doors, consider plain etched glass to complement the paintwork. Etched glass is also a good option for windows, creating a sleek look that is perfect if you want guaranteed privacy without the need for shutters or net curtains.

A word of warning: unless your home is relentlessly modern, try to avoid concrete as it can have a municipal feel, however well designed. A pair of simple, square planters in a lead finish – planted with bay or box cut into neat shapes – will create a neat, symmetrical feel. Try to avoid the mistake that architects make by fitting a large 'statement' door number – it will either date or irritate.

CLASSIC GOOD LOOKS

For a more traditional look, stick to the classic option of brass. Where possible, retain the original door furniture – even if you're changing the door. If you're not changing the door, make sure that it has a perfect paint job that is shinier than a squaddie's toe caps. A pair of carriage lamps either side of the front door will create an impressive period welcome. Granite sets and terracotta path edging also create a lovely, elegant feel. Even if you're a very keen gardener, try to keep planting and shrubbery to the bare minimum.

STYLE UNDERFOOT

Like flooring inside a house, the materials that you choose for drives, paths, steps and parking spaces are a key part of your 'outside decoration'. There are two options: either go for something simple and serviceable such as gravel with attractive edging or push the boat out with the best quality materials that you can afford. The path that you should avoid at all costs is the 'half-way house option' of reconstituted stone. This really can ruin the look of a house. If cost is not an issue, consider York stone, granite setts and slate as possible ways to make a striking statement.

If you are considering a major change to the front of the house – e.g. building steps or creating additional parking space, it is worth taking advice from an architect who can also advise on any planning-related issues.

'It is only shallow people who do not judge by appearances.'
OSCAR WILDE

Defining idea...

15

How did it go?

Q   **Are there any planning restrictions that govern what you can and can't do to the front of your house?**

A   *Good question. Much depends on the type of house and area you live in. For example, if you live in a listed building in a conservation area, there'll be much tighter controls. Always check with your local planning depart-ment first.*

Q   **I've been told that UPVC window frames are a bit of a turn off for potential buyer.**

A   *Again, much depends on the property. It's not a great idea in a period property but they aren't a problem on newer buildings – or those where low maintenance costs are important, such as holiday homes or rental properties.*

Q   **I like the idea of etched glass but it's expensive and I'm nervous about taking the plunge.**

A   *You can create a remarkably similar effect by sticking sheets of tracing paper in the window. In fact, it's so convincing that you might decide not to bother with the real thing!*

5

The good looking kitchen

**When decorating to speculate, it isn't enough for a
kitchen to be functional – it needs to look good too.**

These days there are dozens of
possibilities — to cater for all tastes and
budgets.

Time was when kitchens had a simple and prosaic purpose, and functional flooring, work tops and sinks were very much the order of the day. But that was when
the role of the kitchen was far more limited than it is today. Fifty years ago, few
visitors to a house would have seen the kitchen – except, perhaps for a glimpse
of it through a serving hatch. Today, it is at the very heart of the home – a multifunctional space used not just for cooking but for a whole range of other activities
including eating, entertaining and doing the laundry.

The result is that we are all much more demanding about the way that a kitchen
looks. The fact that we spend a much greater proportion of our time there – along
with our families and friends – means that we want it to look as visually pleasing as

Here's an idea for you... **Most people think that mood boards are just for living rooms and bedrooms but they are equally useful when planning a kitchen. Collect together the samples or photographs of cabinet materials, furniture, flooring, paint and fabrics to give you an idea of the way that your room will look.**

possible. We now have the same standards for our kitchen as we do for any other 'public' area such as the living room.

There's little doubt then that when adding value to a property, the pressure's on to create a showpiece that functions perfectly *and* looks good too. The styling of kitchens has come on leaps and bounds in the last decade. Previously, the choice was between rustic-looking pine, shaker or something that looked so clinical it wouldn't have looked out of place in an operating theatre.

Today the number of styles on offer has proliferated – and a far greater range of colours and finishes means a far greater number of opportunities for adventurous designs. Follow these steps and you could find yourself in a space that feels more like a glamorous cocktail bar than a kitchen.

TEN STEPS TO A GLAMOROUS KITCHEN

1   Think beyond conventional finishes; there's a new generation of cabinetry in a variety of colours and finishes from high gloss primaries to wonderfully rich, grainy wood and wood effects.

2   Not only is an 'island' unit (a freestanding work surface that sometimes incorporates storage and appliances) a great place at which to work it also separates the cooking area from the eating area. In some cases you might also be able to incorporate a space for informal meals.

3   Consider banishing eye-level cupboards. This creates a much airier, more open look but it will necessitate the creation of more storage elsewhere. If you have sufficient space, try to build a walk-in larder in which ingredients, cooking equipment and crockery are all within easy reach.

4   Cabinets that are supported on legs have a much lighter feel than those that are just mounted on the ground.

5   Good lighting is an essential part of a smart looking kitchen. You can't spend too much money on low voltage spots. Consider hanging a chandelier over the kitchen table for maximum effect.

6   Too often we fall into aesthetic cliché when planning a kitchen – either opting for a rustic farmhouse look or sharp-edged modernity. In particular, be brave

'If you can organise your kitchen you can organise your life.'

Defining idea...

LOUISE PARRISH

with colour. Consider using deep, sophisticated hues such as brown and aubergine – possibly just on one 'feature' wall.

7   The flooring shouldn't be an afterthought. Rather than thinking of it purely in functional terms, choose a striking pattern, colour or texture that draws the whole scheme together.

8   In order for your kitchen to look its best, try to keep the look as pared down as possible. While open shelves are a good way to display favourite china, clutter can look messy – however artfully arranged. A few, well-chosen items will have much more impact.

9   Notice boards seem like a good idea but they soon get clogged up with paper and stop functioning efficiently. If you want to display photographs or artwork, confine it to one particular area.

10   While it is tempting to use a kitchen as a home office, avoid doing so at all costs – file and folders create a chaotic look.

Q   **Glossy finishes and a chandelier in a kitchen? Won't that scare the horses a little? It sounds quite distinctive – and quite at odds with idea of creating a property that appeals to the broadest possible range of tastes.**

How did it go?

A   *Good point – and, yes, you need to ensure that the look keeps on the right side of quirky. But equally, you need to avoid the rather clinical appearance of a show home. A few carefully considered elements that will set it apart from the norm are all that are required ... but don't go mad.*

Q   **But surely a nice, cosy farmhouse style kitchen will tick all the boxes ...**

A   *It depends. At the lower end of the market dominated by melamine it will be a huge pull, but at the higher end the prospective buyer will probably see ten a day.*

Q   **But I love the rustic look ...**

A   *Remember ... it isn't all about you.*

Q   **But don't all these fancy ideas require acres of room?**

A   *No, a glamorous kitchen isn't about space. You can make the smallest galley kitchen look a million dollars if you want – in some senses, it is easier, because you can be more focused on a limited number of elements.*

6

The appliance science

Good appliances speak volumes – but is it really worth paying for an upmarket brand?

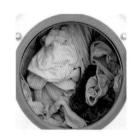

Brands are a shorthand for style, taste and value, so make sure yours say all the right things.

In theory, appliances such as cookers, washing machines and fridges aren't part of your house – they're part of the fixtures and fittings and when you come to sell, you'll only being doing so by separate negotiation (more of which later). And while many of us claim to be unimpressed by such fripperies, almost each and every one of us is impressed by gleaming new appliances, preferably bearing a logo that sounds familiar. An all-singing, all-dancing range cooker is unlikely to clinch a deal but it is an integral part of snaring a buyer.

Remember, too, that buyers love surprises; a small fridge hidden in fitted cupboards in a sitting room or summer house will score significant points.

A BRIEF JOURNEY INSIDE THE PSYCHE OF A POTENTIAL PURCHASER

Even if buyers have their own appliances that they intend to bring with them, 'white goods' as they are known in the trade, are an aspect of a property that bores deep into the subconscious. In their mind's eye there's a very firm link between a rusty old fridge and slovenly behaviour – even if the rest of the kitchen is immaculate. Remember too, that most potential purchasers are either lazy or busy people – or possibly a combination of the two. A good, serviceable appliance already in place is regarded as a huge bonus.

When choosing a low budget appliance, remember that at every price point they all pretty much offer the same features. What is far more important is to make sure that it looks good.

Here's an idea for you...

Research each different type of appliance and compile a list of the main brands with their main features and prices. Decide which are worth investing in heavily – and which aren't. You may decide that it is worth buying an inexpensive fridge (especially if it's out of sight) and invest the saving in a 'statement' item such as a cooker.

LABEL FREAKS

While it isn't worth installing anything more than a basic appliance in modest properties, at the top end of the market there is a breed of potential purchaser for whom top-of-the-range appliances are as dangerously addictive as narcotics. The sight of a gleaming, capacious American fridge with a well known name will prove almost irresistible to some buyers – particularly those who would never dream of actually shelling out for one themselves.

When choosing an appliance it pays to go for a more basic model with a well-known name rather than a mass market brand with all the frills. While it is easy to dismiss the expensive brands as a waste of money, remember that they have a reputation to maintain, so they rarely get it wrong. Again, the exception is in modest properties where cleanliness and functionality are more important than a fancy name.

DISHWASHERS: QUANTITY VERSUS QUALITY

In the kitchen of a large family house you may want to consider buying two inexpensive dishwashers rather than just one. For busy parents producing three meals a day, it means that there is always a good supply of everyday items that never need to be stacked in cupboards. If it seems like an extravagant use of space, remember that it will reduce the amount of cupboard space required elsewhere. And if this still seems like an indulgence, remember that wear and tear will also be reduced by 50 per cent. It's also the sort of touch that will stick in the minds of potential purchasers.

NEGOTIATING A PRICE

Appliances are rarely included in the asking price of a property. Because they are second hand, negotiating a value for them will require a somewhat inexact science. While it might be tempting to include appliances as a bargaining chip in a deal, it may be more profitable to give a specific value, particularly if they are prestige items – and also if replacing them will cause a certain amount of inconvenience. If they are in good condition with plenty of life left in them, the value should be based on how much it would cost to replace them – i.e. what they cost new.

'In designing hardware to be used every day, it was important to keep both the human aspects and the machine in mind. What looks good also often feels good.'
MICHAEL GRAVES, designer

Defining idea...

How did it go?

Q **I'm having difficulty deciding which items I should be prepared to invest the most in. Is there a rule of thumb?**

A *There's an inexact rule of thumb, namely that a desirable cooker will have most allure, followed closely by a stand-alone fridge. However, the value of a famous brand may diminish a little if it is hidden behind doors or in utility rooms.*

Q **Are fridges with water and ice dispensers a good bet?**

A *Yes, in theory, but if you're planning to live with them for long, remember that those on cheaper models have a nasty habit of going wrong. In fact, even expensive models can have a nasty habit of going wrong.*

Q **What about smaller items such as coffee makers?**

A *They are a nice touch but remember that buyers will assume that anything that is easy to remove is unlikely to be negotiated into the price.*

Q **Are white appliances the safest option?**

A *Yes but they can look a bit functional. If appliances are hidden by cabinetry, then it is irrelevant what colour they are. But if they are freestanding, colour definitely has greater impact. However, beware of anything that might be too quirky or fashionable as it might look dated in a few years' time.*

7

Bedded bliss

Never underestimate the allure of a dreamy 'master' bedroom.

A bedroom may represent all that is most private about our lives, but potential buyers will definitely want to take a good look.

Given that we spend almost a third of our lives asleep, it makes a lot of sense to focus a good proportion of our time, thought and effort on creating a great looking, comfortable bedroom. And, in most cases, all that focus will be on just one room – the unfortunately named 'master' suite.

Bedrooms have now joined bathrooms as the main preoccupation for potential buyers (followed a close third by a large but easily maintained garden). Much of the reason for this is down to the influence of hotel rooms that have become increasingly design-led, and leave travellers wanting to achieve the same effect at home. Another new development – and the two are fairly closely linked – is the fact that we have discovered ways to create bedrooms that aren't governed by convention (i.e. the idea that bedside tables, wardrobes and trouser presses are all compulsory).

Now, there are a far greater variety of options – from sleek padded headboards to plantation shutters. And, following the lead of designers, we are learning to use

Here's an idea for you... **Because it is important that a bedroom has the broadest possible appeal, search the internet for images of simply decorated, contemporary hotel rooms that will give you plenty of inspiration for creating a pared down, comfortable look.**

space better, either with streamlined fitted cupboards or by banishing storage to another room completely – perhaps an adjoining dressing room, or a spare bedroom nearby.

With potential buyers in mind, it is essential to focus on one key aspect, whatever style you choose – comfort. A room can be as visually appealing as you like, but if the space doesn't work or the bed isn't comfortable, it is unlikely to appeal to buyers. Remember, too, that a well organised space is more important than the space itself – there's no intrinsic value to having a large bedroom just for the sake of it. In most cases, the space could be much better devoted to storage (i.e. a walk-in wardrobe) or an en suite bathroom.

When choosing a decorating scheme it is important to create a look that has most universal appeal – and one that is in keeping with the style of the rest of the house. Of all the rooms in the house, this is the place where it is important to avoid quirkiness and eccentricity. It is also important to create a scheme that a potential buyer can easily change to suit their own tastes and any furniture that they might have.

CLASSIC BLISS

If choosing a period feel, keep the look fresh and light. Bold 'historic' wallpapers such as Toile de Jouy or chintz might be an essential ingredient in country-style decorating, but many potential buyers will find it hard to see beyond them. It is better to create an updated classic feel with furniture that will leave with you – i.e. a four poster bed, traditional bedside tables and a dressing table. Even then, make sure that they are as simple as possible and opt for light, painted finishes, rather than heavy wood. If choosing elaborate curtains, it is best to choose plain fabrics.

CONTEMPORARY BLISS

For the bed, consider a combination of a divan and tall rectangular headboard upholstered in a textured fabric such as velvet. If space is limited, a good option alternative to a bedside table is a wall-mounted lamp or anglepoise. Blinds create a simple, pared down look but curtains offer better insulation from sound, light and the cold. Curtains with large rivet heading on poles create a sleek appearance – also, consider pelmets that hide the track. Walls should be kept plain – possibly with one in a contrasting hue. If choosing a contemporary wallpaper, try to avoid anything that will look too quirky.

ROMANTIC BLISS

If you are sufficiently confident in your abilities, you can blow potential purchasers away with a room that is designed as a haven. The emphasis, however, should be very much on beauty not quirkiness (the two are often confused but hugely different). You can create a wonderful, escapist fantasy feel with a simple four poster bed, pale floors, walls and either plantation shutters in the windows or sheer curtains. This will have the effect not just of creating a sense of privacy but will cocoon the occupants in a secluded space perhaps with the sense that they have been transported to another world. This all might sound frighteningly cheesy but it can be as effective as big name kitchen in hooking a buyer. Remember, though, that however romantic it might be, practicality is also of the utmost importance.

'Sleep – the most beautiful experience in life – except drink.'

WC FIELDS

Defining idea...

How did it go?

Q The main bedroom in my flat is quite small, can you suggest any nifty space saving ideas?

A *As well as substituting a bedside table/lamp combo for an anglepoise, there are plenty of ways to save space, such as shallow, wall-mounted tables and under-bed storage. But, where possible, banish as much as possible to other rooms.*

Q And how can I make a small bedroom look bigger than it really is?

A *Decorate it in nothing but white – white floors, white walls, white furniture, white bedlinen and white curtains. Add a few accessories (throws, cushions, etc) and you'll have a room that looks smarter than anything twice the size.*

Q Will it help if I buy a smaller bed?

A *No. It's a curious and little recognised fact that large pieces of furniture such as beds, cupboards and chests of drawers actually make small rooms look bigger. It is better to fill a small room with a large bed and nothing else but a couple of wall mounted lights. It is much more comfortable, too.*

Q Surely one of the reasons that hotel rooms look so great is that they aren't filled with clothes?

A *Precisely – that's the reason it is essential that you banish clothes and clutter to another part of the house.*

8
Store and order

You can't create too much storage in a house – it's the secret to creating a calm, ordered feel.

It's not just about having the storage space, though, it's about setting aside the right areas too.

There is one incontrovertible truth about the people who might possibly buy your house. And that is that they *hate* clutter. It isn't that they are necessarily very tidy people themselves – far from it. Many of them live in conditions of unutterable squalor. But that doesn't mean that they find the jumble of other people's lives deeply offensive.

It isn't just discarded clothes, novelty ornaments and collections of obscure beer bottles that bother potential buyers, it is also the paraphernalia of everyday life; CD collections, kitchen accessories and make-up (yes, even in a bathroom). In the houses of others, however, the only place in which these people (even the deeply slovenly, hypocritical ones) wish to see any of these things is neatly stored away in cupboards.

The other fact that you can't escape is that rooms crammed with clutter look much smaller than those that are decorated with just a few items. The following guidelines might seem draconian. After all, houses are for living in. But the purpose of this advice is to make your house as attractive as possible to potential buyers. Remember, *it's not all about you.*

LIVING ROOMS

In living rooms it is a good idea to resist the temptation to create a lot of open storage for books, CDs, picture frames and knick-knacks. While there is no doubt that many people might enjoy looking at photographs of your 21st birthday party and the books that you read on holiday ten years ago, there is no escaping the fact that the effect can kill a room. If you have a large collection of books, keep them in a home office or, failing that, in boxes. A few photograph frames and decorative accessories might help create a personal feel but keep them to a minimum and edit them heavily.

Here's an idea for you... **If you're preparing a property for sale and want to create a simple look, consider 'decanting' any extraneous possessions into a commercial storage unit; it is surprisingly inexpensive and you'll find the results mind-blowing.**

For a sleek, contemporary look, consider a long, low sideboard in which items such as music systems, CDs and DVDs can be stored.

KITCHENS

Hanging pots, pans and kitchen implements from the ceiling and cramming a dresser full of china might create a charming rustic feel, but it will make your kitchen look like a junk shop. If you have a dresser, a collection of plates in matching or complementary colours is the best option, otherwise stow all tableware and cooking equipment well out of sight.

BEDROOMS

In the main bedroom, try to store clothes elsewhere – for example, in a spare room or home office. Failing that, opt for sleek fitted storage, rather than a free-standing cupboard. If space is severely limited, consider under-bed storage trays on runners but make sure that they are hidden from view with a simple, tailored valance.

BATHROOMS

Fitted 'vanity units' that enclose the space under the wash basin offer the most effective use of available room. However, there also tends to be plenty of dead space above the bath and in alcoves which, however shallow, can provide useful storage. Where possible 'closed storage' (i.e. cupboards with doors) will create a look that is sleeker and more pared down than open shelves and niches.

HOME OFFICES

After the kitchen, this is the room where well-planned storage is essential. However, unlike most rooms, try to avoid 'closed' storage (i.e. any item of furniture with doors) which makes files much more difficult to find. The secret of good looking 'open' storage is to create order with neatly labelled file holders and storage boxes that are all the same colour.

'A place for everything.
Everything in its place.'
BENJAMIN FRANKLIN

Defining idea...

HALLS AND LANDINGS

Ideally, it is best to keep these areas clear unless a property has very little storage space. However, look out for alcoves and niches that can be used for fitted shelves – floor to ceiling are the best.

ATTICS

Loft spaces are the traditional option but ensure that the area is clean and dry and as easily accessed as possible. If items that you have stored are too hard to find, you'll never seem them again. Good storage is about being able to take items out as well as put them away.

OUTBUILDINGS

Many houses – particularly those in rural areas – have outbuildings that allow you to create long term storage. But ensure that this isn't a shambles; any outbuilding needs to be dry, well-lit and easily accessed – with boxes and shelves clearly labelled.

Q   Are transparent plastic boxes a good bet?

A   They are – but don't be tempted to leave them on display. A storage issue isn't resolved until something has been placed in a cupboard or on a well organised shelf. Storage equipment – from storage boxes to CD racks – are an eyesore.

Q   Isn't there a danger that if you completely empty a room it will look rather bland and impersonal?

A   Yes – and that's not a bad thing either. Too many personal possessions inhibit a potential purchaser from imagining themselves living there. They provide far too much information. Your aim should be to create a look that is as close to that of a developer's show home as possible.

Q   Not even a few photographs?

A   No, not really – the only possible exception are photographs of children, which create the feeling of a happy family home.

Q   Pot plants?

A   No, no, no, no! If you want to warm the place up a bit, invest heavily in fresh cut flowers – white are best, and try to avoid marigolds and carnations at all costs.

How did it go?

9

Garden answers

Is a large, elaborate garden a blessing or a curse?

There's more to a garden than a bit of lawn, so make sure that yours attracts buyers like bees to blossom.

There are, very broadly speaking, four different types of garden. Depending on which of the following categories your garden falls into – and the type of house you have – you need to respond accordingly when considering saleability.

THE GARDEN FOR ENTERTAINING

The focus of attention here is a large terrace or expanse of decking that will provide plenty of room for alfresco dining. A large parasol, table, chairs and a few planters are far more important than a lawn or herbaceous borders, which are either minimal or non-existent.

Suitable for: Most small or medium sized properties. Buyers of luxury homes will demand a more striking outlook. Keen gardeners will happily tailor to their own needs.

THE MODERN 'STATEMENT' GARDEN

Increasingly popular in towns, these visions in slate and gravel are all about Zen simplicity, symmetry and serenity. Planting tends to be limited to grasses, bamboo and topiary and the focus will often be a minimalist water feature.

Suitable for: Young city dwellers. Older buyers might find the look too austere/pretentious.

Here's an idea for you... **Once your garden is finished, create a collection of photographs of your house in early spring, when it is a fresh, green and verdant as possible. If you put your house on the market in the autumn or winter you can leave the images in an album for potential purchasers to see. Better still, create a slide show 'loop' on a PC or lap top and leave it in the kitchen.**

THE GARDENER'S GARDEN

These slices of Eden are a heady mix of herbaceous borders, shrubs and picture perfect lawns. Keeping all three can amount to a full time job – even those that are quite small.

Suitable for: Other gardeners. Anyone else may be put off by maintenance issues – particularly those with rolling lawns that can take up to a day to mow.

THE LOW-MAINTENANCE, COUNTRY-STYLE GARDEN

While those areas that are close to the garden might offer a token bed or two and a lawn that that can be mowed in a matter of minutes, the hinterland is devoted to wild flower meadows and an orchard.

Suitable for: Everyone. This garden caters for all tastes, from lazy gardeners not wanting to get their hands dirty to the keen gardeners who are eager to tame the wilderness.

THE BLANK CANVAS

As well as the four main types of garden there is, of course, the blank canvas, which is little more than a patch of turf surrounded by a fence. It is a type of garden that often comes with new development, or a house that has been rented out to tenants.

Suitable for: Everyone – but bear in mind that time poor/lazy buyers may be put off by the challenge and expense of creating a garden from scratch.

THE DANGERS OF THE ECCENTRIC GARDEN

There is a tradition of gardeners using their outside space as a way to express their personalities – this can range from lovingly created collections (gnomes, statuary, antique farm

'Gardening requires lots of water – most of it in the form of perspiration.'
LOU ERICKSON

Defining idea...

39

machinery) to follies and grottoes. However, the same rule applies to the outside of a house as it does to the inside: try to create a look that has universal appeal. While there are some garden features that may add to the charm of a house, they are few and far between. You should think seriously about dismantling any structures that might detract from the overall appearance of the garden.

CREATING A GARDEN THAT PLEASES EVERYONE

When preparing a house for sale, ensure that the garden has the broadest possible appeal. If a garden is too high maintenance, try to rationalise it by filling in some of the beds. If it is too featureless, look for ways to make it more inviting – even if it is with just a few carefully positioned shrubs.

The garden must reflect the lifestyle of the person who will live there. A large family house should have a large child-friendly garden, while a small ground floor flat that is likely to be the first rung on the property ladder needs something simple and low maintenance. However, whatever the size – even if there's barely room to swing the proverbial cat – make sure that there is an area where people can eat out.

Whatever your plan, the two most important issues are tidiness and a well-maintained boundary. If you do nothing else, make sure that the grass is cut and the fence is in good shape.

Q **Because I'm a keen gardener I have created quite an elaborate layout, with a combination of herbaceous borders, shrubs and a vegetable patch. Should I really destroy all my hard work?**

How did it go?

A *No, you should simply try to temper it. Where possible simplify the planting and tidy away any plants in containers that need lots of watering. If there is an area of lawn that you can use as a wild flower meadow, do so.*

Q **But surely a beautiful garden can be a selling point?**

A *Much depends on the property. If it's a beautiful country house then it might be an advantage but even then buyers will have their own tastes and agendas.*

Q **Is it a good idea to create a lot of child-friendly attraction such as climbing frames and a Wendy house?**

A *If you have children of your own who will benefit from them, then do it, but there isn't much point in installing them as bait for a buyer. For families with children the most important thing is that there is are enough open spaces, uncluttered by flowers and that it is possible to make the garden secure.*

Q **There's a high chance that my house will be bought by a buy-to-let landlord. What should I do with the garden?**

A *Make it as low maintenance as possible – if it's small, consider putting down gravel. If it's relatively large, a featureless lawn is all you need.*

10

The ship shape house

When preparing a house for sale you need to do a 'wear and tear' audit.

Flaking paint, broken tiles and trailing wires will all cost you far, far more money than paying someone to sort them out

When you've lived in a property for a few years it's easy to become immune to its failings such as chipped banisters, scuffed skirting and grubby grouting. Yet, however smart the rest of the house, it's precisely those imperfections that will stick out like a sore thumb when the time comes to sell.

'But, but, but …' the more slovenly breed of property speculators will cry, 'surely that's what the smell of freshly ground coffee, cut flowers and baroque music will cover up'. The problem is that they won't – and the more sleek and pared down the interior, the greater the chance that any imperfections will be highlighted.

It is pointless to try to con yourself that prospective buyers will be so charmed by your dog/children/collection of tribal carvings that they won't notice the bottle of red wine that was absorbed by your living room carpet during a riotous party. And any attempts to distract them with moody lighting and eccentric decorative

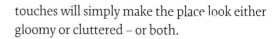

Here's an idea for you... **Much of the problem with 'snagging' is that because a job is small, we think that we won't get someone to come and do the work. Find a good all-round builder who can take on everything from hanging pictures, to fixing a leaking tap and ask them to price the job (rather than paying by the day). Even if you end up paying for the equivalent of three or four days' work, it will be a worthwhile investment.**

touches will simply make the place look either gloomy or cluttered – or both.

There's no doubt that if you are prepared to invest time and/or money, you'll be repaid many times over. There are two good ways to spot flaws. One is to ask someone with a good eye for detail to come and take an objective look round your house and create a 'snagging list' of details that need to be sorted. The other is to take photographs of every room, a process that will highlight imperfections far more effectively than your own naked eye (the camera never, ever lies).

The starting point of any snagging operation is a thorough spring clean. This might sound obvious but it has the benefit not only of improving the look of the place, but also of highlighting any snags that may not already be on your list.

When deciding on a strategy for tackling problems, remember that it is often better to completely replace various elements, rather than to 'make do and mend'. It is better, for example, to replace a stained good quality carpet with a cheap, clean one.

WALLS

- It is worth hanging on to spare paint and wallpaper so that you can do small repairs easily.
- Try to avoid 'spot' painting marks and scratches. It is often easier to simply paint another coat of the same paint.
- If you repaint any part of the house, make it the stairwell – this part of the house tends to have the worst marks. If you're doing more than simply adding a top coat, consider repainting in a very light colour, regardless of your own personal taste.
- Fix any wallpapers that have lifted with wallpaper glue and a seam roller.

FLOORING

- Industrial cleaning will remove general dirt but isn't guaranteed to eradicate deep stains, particularly on light carpets.
- There are all sorts of ways to try an get rid of serious stains, such as patching carpets and covering them with rugs but in many cases it can make more sense to replace it. The other disadvantage of too many rugs is that they make rooms look smaller.

BATHROOM TILES

- Replacing broken tiles – cleaning grouting (or renewing it) is an inexpensive way to revive a tired bathroom.
- Never paint over old tiles – the finish *never* looks as good.

'A small leak can sink a great ship.'

BENJAMIN FRANKLIN

Defining idea...

ELECTRICS

- Grubby old light switches send all the wrong signals. Where possible replace them or, failing that, clean them within an inch of their lives.

UPHOLSTERY

- The same people who try to cover up carpet stains with rugs try to pull the same trick by draping throws all over their grubby upholstery. No one is conned. The only answer to badly stained upholstery is to replace it – even if you go out and by a cheap sofa (often this is cheaper than re-covering a sofa).

OUTSIDE

- It's worth repainting the front door and replacing the door mat if it is worn or threadbare.
- Check for broken or cracked panes of glass.
- If gravel is looking thin, it is worth buying a couple of extra bags.
- Mowing the lawn on the morning of a viewing can do wonders for even the most tired looking garden – even in the depths of winter.

Q   **Is it really worth repainting a room that is likely to be redecorated later?**

A   *Definitely. The way that a house is presented is like packaging. If you open something that is beautifully wrapped, your perceptions of it are likely to be far higher than if it comes in a plastic carrier bag. Besides, we're not talking about a painstaking decorating job – if the paint is in good shape, you'll achieve a lot with a roller and a pot of the same paint that was used to paint the wall in the first place.*

Q   **Surely it's not worth buying completely new upholstery?**

A   *In some cases it might be. Also, you'll be amazed at how cheaply you can buy living room furniture in good condition on eBay or in the local paper. Often sellers just want someone to come and take it away.*

Q   **So, freshly ground coffee and Vivaldi won't help to sell a house?**

A   *They might but only a clean one that is in good working order.*

How did it go?

11

The name game

There is a world of difference between a cheap fitted kitchen and an expensive name brand.

But is it a good investment to fork out for a famous name?

You'll soon discover – if you haven't already – that there are very few hard and fast rules in the property game. It's more complicated than that because there are a large number of rules that apply to all the different types of property on the market. In fact, each and every property offers a completely different set of challenges, and the secret of maximising value is to decide which rules apply to which properties.

Choosing a kitchen is a good case in point. There is no doubting the attraction of a big name, luxury kitchen but the amount of value that it will add to a property depends entirely on the type of property that you are developing.

The most important rule is that there has to be some correlation between the value of the property and the value of the kitchen that you are putting in it. So, for example, there would be as much point putting a luxury kitchen in a modest first time buyer's apartment, as there would be in adding leather seats and alloy wheels to a Reliant Robin.

Here's an idea for you... When making a major investment such as a kitchen, it is essential that you do as much research as you can. It isn't just the kitchens on offer that need to be explored – it is also those that have been fitted by other houses in a similar area and price bracket. It is worth spending time masquerading as a prospective buyer looking at the competition.

Yet even this rule has to be treated with care. Many property pundits cite spurious rules of thumb which they claim will indicate that amount that you should spend on a kitchen. One of these is that you should consider spending around 10 per cent of a property's value on a kitchen. In some cases, this might be the case, but in many it would be an inordinately large sum – even in a very high value property. Remember, too, that you may have a property that has so many other things going for it, that the brand of kitchen you choose is irrelevant. Who cares about some fancy-pants Italian kitchen when a house has views of a beautiful trout stream? The money that you might invest in some big name kitchen brand could pay for a beautiful summer house – or even a guest house – on the water's edge that would add far more to the value of the property.

The following are two hypothetical scenarios. In each case a high value, big name kitchen has been fitted, with two very different sets of results

HYPOTHETICAL EXAMPLE 1: THE BAD INVESTMENT

In the countryside around the pretty town of Trumpton, there is a very low supply of large period houses. Most houses change hands privately, and the price of the few that do come on to the open market tends to be inflated by a bidding war or sealed bids.

Analysis

In this case, a good looking, mid market kitchen is perfectly adequate (you're unlikely to recoup the cost of anything more expensive). However, even in an area where there is high demand, potential purchasers might be put off by a kitchen that they might have to replace.

HYPOTHETICAL EXAMPLE 2: THE GOOD INVESTMENT

In Trumpton itself there are a large number of semi-detached terraced family houses that appeal to families with young children. However, because many people trade up to larger houses there is quite a high turnover of properties, with the result that there is always a choice of three or four properties at any given time.

Analysis

Here, a high value kitchen would not only offer a unique selling point but it would give a very legitimate reason to charge a premium price.

WHY GOOD QUALITY KITCHENS COST MONEY

It is too easy to dismiss big name kitchens as a triumph of salesmanship over substance. While, to the untrained eye, expensive kitchens look dramatically different to cheap ones, you don't need to look too hard to find out why they can cost twenty times more. The

'Mere parsimony is not economy. Expense and great expense, may be an essential part in true economy.'
EDMUND BURKE

Defining idea…

51

combination of handmade joinery, high quality materials and the expertise of the designer means that the two types of kitchen have little in common. However, the question of which is the best investment, depends on where they will end up.

How did it go?   **Q**   **Is there any point in tarting up a kitchen that has begun to look a bit tired?**

      A   *If the finished project will reflect well on the rest of the house, then it is certainly worth considering. Fitting new cupboard and drawer fronts – as well as new work surfaces – on to an existing kitchen is a relatively straight-forward and inexpensive business. But remember that if the configuration is flawed, then there is a limit to what a new look will achieve. Fitting an inexpensive but well-planned kitchen might be a better option.*

      Q   **If working to a tight budget are there any instances in which a cheap kitchen can be fitted in a high value house?**

      A   *Very few. People making a major investment in a house expect a certain number of boxes to have been ticked. If the kitchen is small, and not a selling point, then it may be possible to get away with it. Mid market to upmarket is the best option.*

12

The living is easy

These days, a living room can be used for eating, entertaining, working, playing and relaxing.

A great living room can make a house. Here's how to get it right.

There is no doubt that in large properties the living room has now been eclipsed by the kitchen as the showpiece of a large, family home. It is in large kitchens where most of our relaxing and entertaining takes place, leaving the sitting room with something of an identity crisis. In small properties, the situation tends to be rather different – living rooms often double as dining rooms and in many cases they might have to moonlight as a home office too.

Of all the rooms in a house, the living room tends to be the most multi-purpose. Depending on how you use the room, follow a few basic rules

THE FORMAL LIVING ROOM

This is by far the easiest room to decorate; a sofa – or two – and a couple of armchairs arranged round a focal point such as fireplace is all that is required. It is important, however, that the furniture doesn't crowd the room – there needs to be plenty of room between individual items and cramming furniture against the wall is never a good look. It is also the easiest room in which to make a style statement. For maximum appeal, keep the backdrop muted with just a dash of pattern and 'accent' colour (i.e. a variety of accessories in a co-ordinating hue). Also, where possible, keep clutter to a minimum – no massed ranks of photograph frames and collections of ceramics. If this sounds simple, that's because it is.

THE LIVING ROOM/MEDIA ROOM

Similar to the formal living room but in its midst there will be an enormous television lurking. Beware of large plasma screens that can dominate small rooms – and look out of place in a traditionally styled space. In the absence of a dedicated media room a small screen that can be hidden away is the best bet. Alternatively, in a double ended living room, have the television at one end and the entertaining area at the other.

THE LIVING/DINING ROOM

Unless you have a large, 'double ended' living room (the sort found in Victorian and Edwardian houses) it might be best to incorporate a large round table in the scheme that will serve as an impromptu dining table. If, however, the result looks like a overfilled furniture shop, consider the option of a folding table or one that can be used as a desk (see below).

Here's an idea for you... **After a kitchen, the room that requires the most detailed planning is a living room – particularly one that fulfils a variety of different functions. Scale drawings of the space itself – as well as major items of furniture (both existing and potential) will help focus your mind on getting the right configuration. Like all the best designs, it is essential that form follows function.**

THE LIVING ROOM/HOME OFFICE

With the advent of the laptop computer, it is much easier to use the living room as an office. An occasional table – or a small folding dining table – that can double as a writing desk can easily be incorporated into the scheme. Try to be disciplined about filing – and if possible keep it in a cupboard or on bookshelves.

THE LIVING ROOM/PLAY ROOM

This combination is rarely an ideal marriage but the key is storage, storage and more storage. The ideal layout is a 'double ended' living room in which in half is devoted to the playroom. If there are any alcoves, try if possible to put in some fitted storage.

THE MULTI-PURPOSE LIVING ROOM

In very small properties, there is chance that a living room will have to fulfil all the above functions. If so, tidiness is essential and where possible try to keep the room as spare as you can.

Classic good looks

When planning the style of a room it never pays to go too far in one particular direction. The classic look still has a broad appeal but it is a mistake to create a space that someone with contemporary tastes will find difficult to imagine changing. The best recipe includes furniture with simple shapes and classic fabrics in a muted palette of colours. Also, avoid the temptation to accumulate too much clutter – or if you do, be prepared to put it away before you come to sell.

Cool and contemporary

'*There is nothing like staying at home for real comfort.*'
JANE AUSTEN

Defining idea...

The modern look has the advantage of making rooms look larger than they actually are. It is particularly suited to small spaces as it relies on just a few key pieces. In the same way that it is important that classic interiors don't look too cluttered, it is essential that the contemporary schemes don't look

55

too cold and masculine. The best antidote to masculinity is fabrics with plenty of pattern and texture – even if it is limited to a few cushions on a sofa.

PREPARING A LIVING ROOM FOR A SALE

This is the room that will benefit the most if you choose to hire a storage unit. While you need to make it clear what role the room plays (i.e. dining, home office, play room) with a few token items, try to remove everything that isn't completely necessary.

How did it go?

Q **I have a small house where it is essential that I fit storage in the living room. Do you have any advice?**

A *A large, all-in-one storage unit is cheaper than fitted cupboards but won't necessarily make the best use of the space, particularly if space is at a premium. Whichever you choose, remember that closed storage will create a much calmer, more pared down feel than open shelves.*

Q **What are the other storage options in a living room?**

A *Chests with lids can be used as side tables – and coffee tables can be used as storage, too.*

Q **What is the best approach to storage in a large living room?**

A *If it's a large living room in a large house, I'd try to keep storage out of the equation altogether.*

13

Flooring

Flooring isn't just about functionality – it's an intrinsic part of a decorative scheme.

Whether you're considering a comfy carpet or polished parquet, a quality underfoot experience is one of the essentials.

While many people think of flooring as a finishing touch, it is as key to the look of a room as the walls and furniture. And it's more than just a purely functional ingredient, too; in a simple, contemporary environment, it offers a way to add warmth and texture. Nevertheless, the starting point of the decision-making process should always the purpose that the floor will serve.

FLOORING OPTIONS

- *Fitted carpet.* The term covers a wide range, from utilitarian nylon beloved by student landlords, through to those with a wonderfully deep pile that feels luxurious underfoot.
  Pros – Much more comfortable and quiet than other types of flooring.
  Cons – Unless very well-maintained, it can trap dirt and dust. In the long term, cheap carpet isn't as durable as hard flooring such as wood, stone or terracotta. Stains are another drawback.
  Uses – Ideal in bedrooms and living rooms – and anywhere that babies are likely to be crawling.

- *Rugs.*

  Pros – Easier and generally cheaper to replace than fitted carpet.

  Cons – They need to be combined with another type of floor, ideally wood, stone or terracotta. Too many small rugs make a room look messy – and on hard floors they have a tendency to slip and trip you up.

  Uses – Ideal anywhere you want to add colour and texture to a scheme – and also if you want to add warmth to a hard floor.

- *Natural flooring.*

  Pros – Sisal, seagrass and coir have become popular in recent years as a more contemporary alternative to carpet with more texture and rugged looks.

  Cons – Not as durable as hardwood flooring.

  Uses – Anywhere that you would use carpet but some fitters are reluctant to lay some varieties in stairs because it can be slippery.

Here's an idea for you... **Start a large collection of flooring samples that you can compare side by side. Also, when you are creating a 'mood board' of fabric, paint and wallpaper that you are considering for a scheme, remember to include samples that work well with the colour and texture of the rest.**

- *Wood.*
  Pros – Durable, smart and low maintenance.
  Cons – Good quality wooden floors can be ruinously expensive. They can also be extremely noisy, particularly for downstairs neighbours.
  Uses – Excellent in halls and kitchens. In living rooms and bedrooms you may want to combine them with rugs.
- *Laminate.*
  Pros – This is a low cost option that has a similar look and feel to wood.
  Cons – Cheaper versions aren't especially durable and like wood they can also be noisy.
  Uses – Anywhere you would use wood.
- *Vinyl.*
  Pros – Often confused with linoleum or 'lino' (see below), this is a functional product that also has the advantage of coming in a huge range of colours and patterns – that often mimic other materials such as stone or wood.
  Cons – Cheaper versions look mass produced and are not as durable as other types of flooring (nevertheless they are cheap to replace).
  Uses – Kitchens and bathrooms.
- *Linoleum.*
  Pros – A durable, natural product made from a combination of cork and resin that comes in a wide range of colours, often with a slightly marbled texture. Ideal if you want to create simple graphic patterns.
  Cons – It can be expensive.
  Uses – Kitchens and bathrooms.

'Every calamity is to be overcome by endurance.'
VIRGIL

Defining idea...

59

- *Stone/Terracotta.*
  Pros – Very hard wearing and lends a wonderful texture and colour to a scheme. Ideal for a period look – but also good for contemporary schemes.
  Cons – Expensive and not as comfortable underfoot as carpet and if it has an uneven surface it can be hard to keep clean. In kitchens, remember that glass and china are far more likely to break if dropped.
  Uses – Kitchens, bathrooms, halls and corridors.
- *Concrete.*
  Pros – In modernist homes concrete – either raw or painted – can make a very functional, inexpensive floor.
  Cons – However, while it is well suited to halls and utility rooms, beware of using it too extensively – as even the most hardened minimalist might find it hard to stomach.
  Uses – Halls and playrooms.

UNDERFLOOR HEATING

If you are planning a major flooring project you should consider underfloor heating – particularly for bathrooms and halls. It can be combined with most types of flooring, including wood and carpet.

BUYERS' EXPECTATIONS

In a high value property, buyers will expect stylish, good quality flooring such as wood and stone. In low value properties, they're unlikely to be such a good investment – what is more important is that they are clean and functional; a clean, cheap carpet is better than a marked expensive one.

Q **Surely painted floorboards are the cheapest type of flooring?**

How did it go?

A *In modest properties where boards are in good condition, painting boards is an option. But remember that they are noisy and high maintenance – and for many people they are an acquired taste.*

Q **I like the texture of deep carpet but not the wall-to-wall, fitted look. Can you have carpet made into rugs?**

A *Yes, it is relatively straightforward and inexpensive. You can also have natural flooring such as sea grass and sisal made into rugs. The obvious advantage of this approach is that the rugs can be removed when you move.*

Q **I assume that wood and stone are very expensive to lay.**

A *Indeed. In some cases you may have to make some structural changes. But remember that both should last a lifetime – and send out positive signals to potential buyers. Even using a limited amount of wood or stone – for example, in a hall – you can set the mood for a property.*

Q **Do you have any suggestions for serviceable stone floors?**

A *Slate has a smooth, serviceable surface that is ideal in kitchens. York stone is great for a cottagey look and limestone has a clean, contemporary feel.*

14

The good looking laundry room

When space allows, a dedicated laundry room can be a huge draw to potential buyers

There's far more to it than just keeping your laundry off the kitchen floor.

One of the joys of larger properties is that they offer the luxury of devoting entire rooms – albeit rather small ones in some cases – to functions that in smaller properties get just a corner of a room. In recent years, these rooms have been used as a way to add to the wow factor of a house – for example, as walk-in wardrobes, shower rooms and laundry rooms.

The objective of creating The Perfect Laundry Room – a vision of clean white paint, immaculate surfaces and beautifully organised linen cupboards – is to create the impression that what most people regard as a hideous chore is actually a pleasure. Doing any activity in a environment that is specifically designed for the job is always more pleasing than having to make the best of difficult conditions.

In smaller houses the laundry tends to be done in the kitchen but a space that is dedicated to the washing, drying, ironing – and possibly storage – is enough to make many potential buyers salivate uncontrollably.

LAYOUT

Laundry rooms don't need to be large – and there are plenty of ways to make the best of even the smallest space. The minimum requirement is a couple of base unit cupboards placed side-by-side with a washing machine with wall-mounted cupboards or open shelves that rise all the way to the ceiling (there's no reason to spend much money on these, as wear and tear is minimal). If you wanted to include a tumble drier into this arrangement, you could add a front loading model and place it above the washing machine.

If space allows, include a sink that will provide a place for hand washing – and for washing items such as muddy boots that you may not want in the kitchen. You could also create more storage by having two runs of cabinets that face each other.

There are three essential ingredients in the perfect laundry room:

1   Washing machine (duh!)
2   Lots of storage – not just for laundry but also for all sorts of other items, such as shoe cleaning equipment, tools, cleaning fluids, picnic sets.
3   A wall-mounted fold-down ironing board (these can be hidden in cupboards).

Here's an idea for you...

Strange though it may sound, you'll find all the inspiration you need for laundry room storage in a kitchen showroom. Look at the configurations of drawers, doors and surfaces and work out how you can make the most of the space available.

… and three optional ingredients:

1   A tumble drier
2   Alternatively, you could use the much more eco-friendly option of a long drying rack suspended from the ceiling on a pulley system.

3   If you've room you might be able to sneak a fridge and/or freezer into the corner.

LINEN STORAGE

If room allows, a well planned airing cupboard will gild the lily; for a number of reasons, including the heat that they generate, it is a good idea to combine linen storage with your hot water tank.

THE LOOK

Clean and clinical is the best option; brilliant white paint, white surfaces, white units and an inexpensive vinyl floor, preferably in a large black and white chequer board pattern. The only colour should be in the red cheeks of the overexcited potential purchaser.

JUSTIFYING THE SPACE

While devoting a whole room to laundry might seem like an indulgence, bear in mind the pressure that you'll be taking off the kitchen – out comes the washing machine, tumble drier, ironing board – and you'll also have the benefit of plenty of storage space for items such as cleaning fluids (and even surplus crockery and foodstuffs).

When planning the layout of an existing property – or just a new extension – this is the sort of room that you can create with sufficient thought and planning.

'We should all do what, in the long run, gives us joy, even if it is just picking grapes or doing the laundry.'
EB WHITE

Defining idea…

How did it go?

Q   **I have a room that is big enough to accommodate a washing machine and a tumble drier but little in the way of cupboards and surfaces. Do you think I have any chance of creating a utility room in such a small space?**

A   *Consider stacking the tumble drier on top of the washing machine – or vice versa. Also, a wall-mounted ironing board will make best use of all the available space.*

Q   **Is it possible to have an 'open plan' laundry room that is part of the kitchen but which has its own dedicated function?**

A   *Yes – although this doesn't offer all the benefits of a dedicated laundry room, it can be a good solution if space is limited – or if you want to make the most of all the available light and don't want an unnecessary wall.*

Q   **Are there any other rooms that will accommodate the functions of a utility room?**

A   *Yes, plenty. In rural areas, where a room in which wet outdoor clothes and boots can be stored, it is possible to create a space where a 'boot room' and a utility room can be quite happily joined together. This is also a good place to fit the central heating boiler. In addition, a multi-purpose space such as this is also a great place for extra storage and for the dog to sleep. Some people even fit a shower, as this provides the perfect space for the wet and muddy to get clean and warm before venturing into the rest of the house.*

15

Office politics

Because more of us are working from home, a well-planned home office will win the hearts of buyers.

The most important criterion for successful home working is a space that is conducive to relaxed concentration.

In the beginning was the study, the gloomy book-lined refuge where the pipe smoking Victorian man of the house would read newspapers and write letters. One thing he rarely did in his study was work. But with the advent of the computer, there is a more seamless divide between our personal and professional lives; telephone, PCs and the internet have opened up our homes to the world of work. The result is that many potential buyers will be looking for a functional, attractive, resolved space in which they can envisage themselves spending a working day. Even those who don't work at home will be attracted to the idea of a place where they can use the internet, store books and filing and work on any personal projects that they might have.

Here's an idea for you...

The best designed offices are those we work in. Try to do some research in your own – or a friend's. It should offer a useful illustration of how every square centimetre can be put to good use – and how you may not need as much room as you think.

The ingredients of the perfect home office.

1   *Peace.* In a large family house, the ideal location for a home office is safely away from any busy and noisy roads. For those who work at home full time, an office in an outbuilding is ideal, but otherwise a room that is near bedrooms or in a roof extension is ideal.

2   *Light.* Working in natural light isn't just easy on the eyes, it's also good for the soul. As well as a good desk light, a good even overhead light – low voltage spots are ideal – will make retrieving books and documents easier.

3   *Storage.* This is key; it is essential that the storage is open rather than behind closed doors which makes it time consuming to find books and documents and books in a hurry.

- Unless you're creating a 'show piece' home office on the ground floor, there is little point in investing huge amounts of money in fancy joinery; it is far more important to include the maximum amount of storage that the space will allow and fit as much floor-to-ceiling shelving as possible.
- Try to avoid freestanding shelving – it never makes the best use of the space.
- Even if you fit 'off the peg' shelving it is worth employing the services of a good carpenter to help you plan the configuration and then fit it.

- When planning the layout of a home office, ensure that items that you need to access regularly are within easy reach, preferably from your chair.
- Storing files and brochures in white file boxes will make items easier to find and create a calm, cohesive feel.

4   *Functionality.*
- Choose a chair with castors that allow you to move without having to stand up.
- Castors operate more efficiently on a hard surface such as wood, laminate, vinyl or linoleum.

5   *Good looks.* While this is a functional space it is also important that it will be a pleasant environment. If space allows try to hang some framed prints or photographs on the wall.

THE COMPROMISE HOME OFFICE

In some cases you may have to combine the function of home office with some other room such as a dining room or spare bedroom. If so, try and limit storage to one large fitted cupboard, possibly integrating a pull-out desk.

THE 'REMOTE' HOME OFFICE

While creating a home office in an outbuilding or creating a stand-alone office in the garden might seem expensive, remember that it frees up another room inside the house and offers a quieter, more tranquil environment in which to work. The cost of a pre-fabricated garden office may also be much cheaper than you think.

'Nothing interferes with my concentration. You could put on an orgy in my office and I wouldn't look up.'
ISAAC ASIMOV

Defining idea...

Q   Given the advent of lap tops and wireless technology, is it really worth investing so much money in a home office?

A   *Good question; it could be regarded as something of an indulgence. Much depends on the space you have at your disposal. If there's room to spare, there's no doubt that there is something very luxurious about having a space dedicated to working, e-mailing, using the internet and storing all your books and filing. However, like so many of the added extras (walk-in wardrobes, en suites, laundry rooms, etc.) you simply have to evaluate which best suit the needs of your target market. Also, remember that the functions of a home office are easily incorporated into some other room.*

Q   But if I go for the 'virtual' home office idea, where do I put all my filing, books, hard drives, etc?

A   *You'll be amazed how much you squeeze into a well planned cupboard – you'll also be amazed at how much you don't use on a daily, monthly or even yearly basis. There is a huge amount of what people keep in home office that could easily be stored away – as is the case in a normal office.*

Q   Is a home office a major attraction to buyers?

A   *Yes, particularly if there is plenty of room and it's not taking up space that could be used for something more valuable. If a home office is occupying a bedroom in a four or five bedroom house, you may want to create a room that could easily be converted into its former purpose – or possibly create a bedroom/home office.*

16

The great outdoors

Making the most of outbuildings will offer a range of benefits to buyers.

Not only that — in the meantime you can enjoy the benefits yourself!

Tired or redundant outbuildings or extensions never look great during a house viewing. If they need money invested in them, many potential purchasers make a mental note to consider knocking them down.

How very wrong they are; while a number of outbuildings, particularly those that are attached to listed buildings can be a drain on resources, they also have the potential to offer useful extra space for home offices, guest accommodation, granny flats, play rooms and laundry rooms. They might even offer a useful source of extra income.

When selling a house it is essential that the purpose of an outbuilding is resolved – even if it is just as a watertight storage facility. Alternatively, you may consider getting architects' plans – and planning approval – for some other use.

The top ten uses for a redundant outbuilding or extension:

1   *Utility room.* In the country it is essential to have an all-purpose room near the back door where you can store coats, boots, garden equipment and all sorts of miscellaneous stuff that doesn't have an obvious place in the house. If the room is large enough you could consider combining it with a laundry room (see below).

2   *Laundry room.* A room dedicated to washing, drying and ironing is a great luxury. A laundry room could be in a building that is separate from the main house but ideally it should be attached.

3   *Home office/Studio/Workshop.* An outbuilding is an ideal location for a home office – particularly for those who work at home full time. If there is plenty of natural light, creative types will see as it a good opportunity for artistic endeavours. It is a good idea not to customise the space too much to your own needs; as long as it is warm and dry and there are sufficient electrical points, heating and lighting, potential buyers will be able to adapt it to their own use. If you have the space and budget a WC and a small kitchen are worth considering.

4   *Play room.* Ideally this room should be part of the main house but it is still possible to have a stand-alone playroom – or one that is adjacent to a garage. The only requisites are that it is dry and warm – and there are electrical points.

Here's an idea for you...

If you have enough space for independent accommodation, scour the local property ads for how much it might be worth if it was developed and rented out. Even if you wouldn't want the hassle of a tenant, someone else might and they may be prepared to pay a higher price for the property on the basis of its commercial value.

5   *Entertaining room.* If you don't have the budget for a full restoration of an outbuilding, you could consider simply turning it into a room for occasional entertaining and children's parties. It should be reasonably dry and have plenty of natural light and it can be lit with stand-alone gas heaters. You could also use the room as a storage facility (see below).

6   *Storage facility.* This is another useful role for an outbuilding that requires little investment other than ensuring that the space is dry.

7   *Guest room.* An outbuilding offers a cheap way to add another bedroom and bathroom that is ideally suited to guests. The bathroom need not be elaborate – a shower, WC and a small hand basin are all that is required. Some potential buyers will be attracted to the idea of offering B&B accommodation.

8   *Rentable accommodation/granny flat.* If there is sufficient room, there are many buyers who will be attracted to independent accommodation for an elderly relative or domestic staff such as a carer or au pair. If the flat is suitable for renting, many buyers will take the extra income into account when making financial calculations – when interest rates are low the rent from a small flat can service a significant proportion of a mortgage.

9   *Garden store.* This can be anything from a former privy to an old stable. It is ideal for properties with a large garden. It is worth considering installing a good concrete floor, lighting and plenty of locks (garden theft is a thriving industry in rural areas).

10 *Gym/pool.* A large outbuilding will make a great place for both of the above. Even if you can run to a full-scale pool, consider putting in a hot tub too.

'The time to repair the roof is when the sun is shining.'
JOHN F KENNEDY

Defining idea...

Q   **Surely I'd never recoup the cost of restoring a derelict building?**

A   *It really depends on the project – and what you might use the building for. If it means that you're freeing up a great deal of space in the house by building a home office and creating extensive storage, then it's possible that you could create extra room for a kitchen or a bedroom in the main house.*

Q   **What's the best way to weigh up the different options?**

A   *If you don't have one already, create a scale drawing of your property that includes any outbuildings. When trying to apportion space to different rooms treat the outbuilding in the same way as any other room. You'll soon see how the outbuilding will fit into the bigger picture.*

Q   **What planning and building regulations govern outbuildings?**

A   *If you're planning any changes to an outbuilding, it is essential that you check with your local planning department. If the property is listed, the controls may be even tighter.*

17

Raising the roof

Your attic may be an untapped source of invaluable space.

So why not get up there right now and start dreaming the future.

In the last 20 years or so, architects have become pretty crafty about eking every last inch of extra room out our homes. It's no mean feat – particularly in semis and terraces where there is a limit to how far you can extend. In many cases, the only way is up; a roof extension offers a cost effective way of adding a significant amount of extra floor space.

There are two ways to create a roof extension; one involves making an attic habitable by laying a solid floor, creating walls and adding roof lights or dormer windows. While this is a relatively inexpensive project, it relies on there being sufficient height to create enough standing room. The other, more common – and more costly – option is to raise the roof line to create a room that has as much height as any other room in the house.

Costs of a project such as this will vary according to the size and specification – however, there is no doubt that an investment in a well-planned roof extension with an

Here's an idea for you... **Collect a large pile of interior design magazines and pull out any images of roof extensions that you like the look of. Another good hunting ground is the brochures and websites of companies that sell windows and blinds for roof extensions. The gallery section of interior design websites should also yield suitable images.**

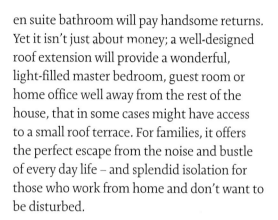

en suite bathroom will pay handsome returns. Yet it isn't just about money; a well-designed roof extension will provide a wonderful, light-filled master bedroom, guest room or home office well away from the rest of the house, that in some cases might have access to a small roof terrace. For families, it offers the perfect escape from the noise and bustle of every day life – and splendid isolation for those who work from home and don't want to be disturbed.

There are a variety of different ways to raise the height of a roof – some better than others. For a number of reasons it makes sense to hire an architect with plenty of experience of similar projects to draw up plans and help with any planning issues. Any raised roof extension will have a significant impact on the appearance of the house, so it is important that the roof line and windows are sympathetic. As well as hiring an architect who is experienced in this type of work, you should also seek out a builder who understands the structural implications – particularly in relation to keeping out the elements. Unless a roof extension is sufficiently water tight, it can cause years of expensive misery.

FURNISHING A ROOF EXTENSION

While they offer a wonderful airy haven away from the rest of the house, once constructed, a roof extension can present quite a design challenge; sloping walls and ceilings create an awkward space that needs taming, ideally with one calming colour. In period houses many people solve the problem by decorating the wall with a busy floral but remember that these are an acquired taste, so tread with care.

Another good way to approach the awkward angles is to fit floor-to ceiling cupboards on one, if not two sides of the room.

The other challenge is the windows which, like the walls and floors, tend to be an awkward shape. In most cases the simplest answer is a roller blind that is fitted into a cassette. However, in many instances only quite thin fabric is fitted to these. You may also want to consider roman blinds or plantation shutters.

THE ONLY WAY IS UP

If you already have an en suite bedroom and a home office you may be asking yourself if there really is any point in converting the roof space. But the chances are that a potential purchaser will be able to put it to good use. And don't forget that the demands of a potential buyer may well be different from yours – they might love a multifunctional space that could be used as a play room or a teenagers' hang out.

'I've always believed the greater danger is not aiming too high as too low.'
PETER SCOTT

Defining idea...

77

How did it go?

Q **For me, the most obvious reason not to create a roof extension is because it will mean that I lose a huge amount of very useful storage. Is there any way round this?**

A *There is no doubting the fact that roof extension has far more value than storage – both to you in the short term and to the long term value of the property. There are two solutions to your problem. One is try to create storage somewhere else in the house that will help to redress the balance, the other is to consider renting a unit in storage facility.*

Q **I'm having real difficulty coming up with a scheme for a bedroom in such a complex room. Is there a quick fix?**

A *Yes, it is to have everything white – walls, bedlinen, furniture, flooring, the lot. You can soften the look with a few splashes of colour such as pink or aqua. To create interest on the walls you could consider fitting sheets of board that look like 'tongue and groove' panelling. It might sound a bit radical but it is perfect for a bedroom, and will create a wonderful airy haven away from the rest of the house.*

18

Not just for oranges

Conservatories have come a long way since their heyday in the nineteenth century.

These days they can be used as everything from dining rooms to offices.

The two most important luxuries when planning any house or apartment are not a designer kitchen or an indoor pool but maximising both the amount of space and light. The great advantage of a conservatory is that they offer both of these in spades. Today, conservatories are rarely built as a self contained unit and instead they are part of an open plan scheme in which they are an integral part. The most obvious example of this is a kitchen extension where a conservatory adds a light, bright eating area to the existing space.

Yet like any major building project, the addition of an extension should be treated with enormous care. It is essential that you choose the right conservatory to suit your house – and only extensive research will help you find the right one. The first rule is that just because you live in a Victorian house doesn't mean that you have to opt for a Victorian-style conservatory – often something sleek and modern can work far better.

The second rule is that sadly, this is one of those areas where you can't escape the fact that there is a distinct correlation between expenditure and good looks. And to be brutally honest, a cheap conservatory tends to equate to a pretty cruddy result,

Here's an idea for you... **When planning a conservatory, you can't do too much research. There's a huge choice of styles and prices on offer and time spent looking at every option will be repaid handsomely. Look up companies on the internet, too, they can provide plenty of additional inspiration.**

with the result that if you only have a limited budget for a conservatory, you might be better spending your money on something else. Finally, before starting on any project, always check with your local planning department to see whether there are any planning or building restrictions.

Remember that in built up areas you need to consider whether you will be overlooked by neighbours. This is an issue that is important when considering any extension that includes lots of glass – but which is particularly important with conservatories. Don't just consider the current situation – also try to anticipate any changes that a neighbour might make in the future, such as removing trees or fences – or building their own extensions.

THE TRADITIONAL LOOK

There is a huge choice of traditional style conservatories, ranging from synthetic-looking entry level models to elaborate reproductions of original designs. If you are opting for a traditional-looking conservatory, it makes sense to keep the design as simple as possible. It is also better to go for a small, good quality conservatory than a large one that looks distinctly, um, er, tacky.

THE CONTEMPORARY LOOK

On urban houses – both modern and period – a sleek glass cube is often the best option. While the choice is far more limited, you should find a design that will suit both your taste and budget.

The three most popular uses for a conservatory:

1. Conservatory kitchen. It is hardly surprising that the most common reason for building a conservatory is to extend a kitchen – it creates a wonderful, light-filled space that is a pleasure to spend time in.
2. Conservatory dining room. While conservatories are often used to extend a kitchen in order to create a dining area, it can also create a stand-alone space.
3. Conservatory living room. A nice idea in principle but in reality it can be a challenge. During the day too much light can be a menace, while at night it can be hard to make the space seem cosy and intimate, particularly when there is a storm raging outside. Remember, too that in the absence of any solid walls, you won't be able to hang pictures or fix lighting. However, if it is a secondary sitting room that has access to the garden, it can be a delight.

HEATING AND COOLING

It isn't just keeping a conservatory warm that is a problem but keeping it cool. Even in the northern hemisphere, conservatories can get unbearably hot, so in the absence of air conditioning it is essential that you consider hanging blinds and the opportunity to create a through draught. Also consider underfloor heating rather than radiators.

LIGHTING

Because of the absence of wall lights, standard lamps may be necessary. However, in order to avoid too many trailing wires, try to plan these in advance so that the socket and lamp are in suitably close proximity.

'Clarity, clarity – surely clarity is the most beautiful thing in the world.'

Defining idea...

GEORGE OPPEN

How did it go?

Q   Is this another area, like the kitchen, where it's best to pay through the nose for something top-of-the-range?

A   *No, no, no, not at all. While it doesn't make sense to build a cheap conservatory, whatever the value of the house, a mid-range model will be perfectly adequate for most purposes. Only consider investing in a top-of-the-range conservatory if you are developing a top-of-the-range house – and only then, if you feel that it will add significant value.*

Q   How does the cost of a conservatory compare with the costs of an extension?

A   *In some cases they are cheaper, but don't be tempted to build a conservatory just because of cost – your choice should be based on which option will do most to enhance the property.*

Q   I'm a little concerned that while a conservatory is great for summer, they aren't really suited to the winter months.

A   *Don't be. During the winter, spending time in a conservatory is a tonic, even on the dullest of days.*

19

The joy of a home help

Employing the services of an architect might seem like an expensive option, but they might also repay your investment.

It's often helpful to throw some professional light on a potential development and can make all the difference between success and failure.

For most of us, our homes are the biggest investment we'll ever make. It isn't just the initial purchase that is so financially consuming, it's all the associated ongoing costs; the interest payments, the endowments, the maintenance, the insurance, etc. But these are costs that we happily pay, not just because they put a roof over our heads but because we know that if we play our cards right we should get a healthy return on our investment. But given all these facts, it is extraordinary how many homeowners are reluctant to seek the help of architects when making major changes to their homes – people who happily shell out huge amounts to other professionals such as car mechanics and dentists.

Here's an idea for you... **Ask friends and acquaintances for any recommendations they might have when choosing an architect. Personal recommendations are much more important than endorsement from professional associations.**

There is something intangible about the nature of an architect's work that makes us strangely reluctant to employ their services. Yet there are few projects, from reconfiguring the layout of rooms, to building an extension, that an architect won't enhance; not just drawing up plans but also finding ways to improve the way that rooms function. Yet the greatest skill of good architects is their capacity to maximise space and light which can completely transform even the most ordinary home. Yes, to non-architects it might sound a bit a bit airy-fairy, but you only need to see the effect that they can have on a property to fully appreciate their worth.

The relationship between architect and client is one where enormous clarity is required. Never assume anything; every aspect of a project has to be agreed in painstaking detail. Also, wherever possible try to use real examples as the basis for your discussion. While technology means that it is possible for architects to create complex, three-dimensional images, nothing will help you to visualise an idea more clearly than photographs of an existing project – or even a visit to one. Try to collect together as many real examples of what it is that you want to create.

There is even a theory among many developers that a good architect will not only help you avoid expensive mistakes but also save you money by suggesting solutions and materials that are cheaper than either you or your builder could have specified. And then there are all the other aspects of a job that they can help with, from preparing planning applications, complying with building regulations as well as recruiting and negotiating with builders.

The extent to which an architect is involved in a project is entirely up to you. At the most basic level you can ask for a set of plans and then take over the rest of the job. Alternatively an architect can be as intimately involved as you'd like them to be. One advantage of using an architect to advise on planning applications is that they are likely to have good on-going relationships with local planning officers. Remember, too, that in the early stages you'll keep costs under control if you don't ask for lots of detailed plans at an early stage – plenty of communication will help you to a resolve options early on.

There's no escaping the fact that architects charge fees that at first glance might seem hefty for a few plans and calls to your local planning office. But that is rather like begrudging your accountant for filling in your tax return. The fact is that you are paying for years of training, expertise and experience – and a good architect can make or break a successful project. Fees are based on their time or on a percentage of the cost of a project. It is essential that your starting point is a full and frank discussion of how their charges are structured – and that you also do research into recent projects that practice has worked on. Ideally, you should try to see the project – or if this is difficult, to examine any work that they may have carried out on their own home or professional premises.

'An expert is a man who has made all the mistakes which can be made in a very narrow field.'

NIELS BOHR

Defining idea...

How did Q **Surely if an architectural practice was any good, it would be**
it go? **working on new build projects, rather than designing exten-**
sions?

A *Point one – there are a lot of terrible architects who build new build-*
ings from scratch. Point two – there is surprisingly little work in new build
projects; most new homes are built to identikit plans on housing estates.
Point three; in many instances it is far more difficult to build a good exten-
sion that works with an existing structure – or successfully re-configure a
house – than build a completely new house.

Q **How can you further convince me that an architect could save me**
money?

A *You'd be amazed. One area that they are particularly helpful is in specifying*
materials and making suggestions for cheaper alternatives. For example,
if an architect persuaded you that a painted concrete floor was perfectly
adequate in a utility room – when you might have chosen something far
more expensive – you will have saved a significant amount of money to set
against that fees. But using an architect isn't just about saving money – it's
also about enhancing value.

20

Shower power

Showers fit into small spaces but they make a huge selling point.

After all, where washing is concerned it's a question of the more the merrier — no one likes to have to queue for the bathroom!

Time was when opportunities to wash and shower were limited to just one room – the bathroom. However, in recent years, the evolution of plumbing technology means that it's easy to fit a shower almost anywhere you choose. So what's the appeal? The most obvious attraction is that each additional shower that you fit will take the pressure off the main bathroom.

In smaller family homes this might mean that you won't have to set aside time, space and money for creating a second stand-alone bathroom. Instead, you could consider simply dividing the functions of one dedicated bathroom and a shower room (or cubicle) and a separate WC. What's more, there is another advantage in adding extra showers to a property in that they offer more privacy, to both you and your guests.

If you feel that a property needs another shower but that there isn't an obvious place to accommodate one, look at a scale plan of the internal space. Remember that adding a stud partition to create a shower room is relatively inexpensive process.

When choosing a site for a new shower, it pays to think laterally. This is especially true in small cottages where space is at a premium but where you may have unused areas in passages and on landings. Wherever you fit a shower, remember that you will save yourself time and money ensuring that the area is as watertight as possible.

Here are some scenarios that you might like to consider:

IN A BEDROOM

If you don't have sufficient space for an en suite bathroom you could consider simply fitting an enclosed shower in one of the corners – and, ideally, a WC in an adjoining or adjacent room. If there's carpet on the floor, ensure that you choose a very efficient shower enclosure.

IN A WC OR CLOAK ROOM

Because all the necessary services are on hand, this is an ideal place to fit a shower room. The chances are that you'll also have a floor that is suited to the purpose.

IN A UTILITY ROOM/LAUNDRY ROOM

If space allows, this is a logical location for a shower. If possible, it should be located near a back or front door, particularly in the country or near the sea where those who are wet and muddy after outdoor pursuits can undress and shower without walking through the rest of the house. The proximity of a washing machine and tumble drier and/or drying rack will mean that dirty and wet clothes can be dealt with immediately.

IN A 'WET ROOM'

Another option to consider is to create a 'wet room' in which there is a WC, basin and shower but no shower enclosure – just very well sealed walls and a floor that is angled so it will drain efficiently. This is a project that needs to be properly researched and, ideally, designed and executed by a company that has experience in this type of work. The advantage is that it makes a good use of space but, for most, it is an acquired taste – perhaps best suited to contemporary houses aimed at younger buyers.

OFF A PASSAGE

When reconfiguring the layout of a house, it is worth having in the back of your mind any opportunities to create a small shower. Inevitably there will be space created by moving walls and services that will present the opportunity to add a shower – an inexpensive way to make use of a few square feet. Ideally

'Water, air, and cleanness are the chief articles in my pharmacy.'
NAPOLEON BONAPARTE

Defining idea…

the space that the shower adjoins should have a water resistant floor such as stone, terracotta, linoleum or vinyl. If there isn't room for a door, remember that you can hang a sturdy shower curtain instead.

HI TECH GIZMOS TO CONSIDER

While in upmarket properties, showers with high power pumps – or 'power showers' – are considered virtually a basic requirement, there are now all sorts of other features to choose from. In the last decade, leaps and bounds in shower technology mean that there are now far more options available. These include:

- Digital control systems that regulate the temperature of the water – some of which can be controlled from outside the shower enclosure (so that you don't get wet – or scalded – while trying to get the temperature right).
- Multi-function shower heads.
- Steam/water combinations.
- Built-in directional massage side jets.
- Aromatherapy dispensers.
- In-shower music systems.
- Colour therapy lighting systems.

All of these features can do a great deal to lift a bathroom above the ordinary.

Q **What's the ideal number of showers that a property should have?**

How did it go?

A *If there's only one bathroom, it is very useful to have at least one, even in a small property. In a four bedroom house, the ideal is two – one upstairs and one downstairs. But remember that any additional showers are luxuries, rather than necessities – it's not worth compromising some other elements in order to create one.*

Q **If space is tight can you ever substitute a shower for a bathroom?**

A *Only in studio flat and secondary accommodation. Always try to fit a bath, even if it's a small one. It's not just about personal taste, it's about the way that a property will be perceived.*

Q **You sound slightly wary about wet rooms – are you?**

A *As a concept, they are slightly in their infancy and might just be a passing fad. However, in the right type of property, a wet room can be a big attraction.*

21

The joys of a simple life

When preparing a property for sale it essential that it isn't cluttered with the paraphernalia of everyday life.

An elegant emptiness will allow viewers to fantasise about how their new dream house will look once they've moved in.

For years, style dictators have tried their best to brainwash us into believing that we should all live in homes that look like nothing more than a succession of empty white boxes. Yet for most of us their standards have been impossible to live up to. And nor would be want to; it requires huge amounts of work to keep a minimally decorated house looking that way and it is a way of life that is hopeless for anyone with small children or pets. The look is only practical for someone who wants to live the life of an ascetic monk.

Like communism, minimalism was a nice idea that never worked out in the real world. Yet, like communism, there are aspects of it that have been very useful in shaping the way that we live. While it is clearly ridiculous to try to live a normal life with all your possessions hidden well out of sight, also it is equally ridiculous try to live a normal life with your possessions cluttering every inch of available space. Clut-

Here's an idea for you... **If you need evidence of the effect that a good de-cluttering session can have on a room, take some photographs of it before and after you begin the process. Not only should this demonstrate the amazing impact that the exercise can have on a room but also that it takes quite a lot to make a room look minimal.**

ter gathers dust and makes it almost impossible to keep a room clean. But, most importantly, it doesn't do anything to enhance the look of a room. As such, clutter is a mortal threat to the value of a property.

Much of the problem lies in the fact that most potential buyers find it almost impossible to see beyond the clutter. Your living room may contain great looking furniture and superb paint schemes, but what the buyer will see is the collection of decorative boxes, the family photographs and the paperweight. And they really shouldn't have to. Most buyers are in a hurry – they want to see the essential elements of a property looking at its best, so that they can come away with a clear impression of what it looks like. They don't especially want to leave with images of your graduation and your nephew's first birthday. If you were hoping to sell you'd car you'd be more likely to empty it before a viewing, rather than treating a potential buyer to the sight of your road maps, CD collection and golf clubs.

Prior to a sale there are three stages in the de-cluttering process that a property must be subjected to.

STAGE 1: THE BIG CHUCK OUT

Do yourself a favour – and one that you should have done long before you decided that the time was right to move. Have a ruthless campaign against old clothes, newspapers, books and toys that haven't been used for years and are unlikely to be used again. Try going to a car boot sale – you'll be amazed at how therapeutic the process can be.

STAGE 2: THE LONG TERM DE-CLUTTER

If preparing a property for sale, it is worth identifying an area where you can create long term repository for clutter. Attics, cupboards and garages are all good options but make sure that once you've de-cluttered, you don't turn any of these areas into an eyesore in the process.

It is worth considering hiring a unit at a local storage facility where you can decant all the extraneous possessions that you can do without while the property is on the market. You'll be amazed at how much you can get rid of in this way – after all consider how few possessions you can survive with when you are on holiday.

STAGE 3: THE QUICK FIX DE-CLUTTER

Before the arrival of a potential buyer, you should create a routine that involves tidying away all essential items that aren't part of the idealised image of the property that you want to project. The house needs to look calm and tidy – but, equally, you don't want it to appear as though it has been burgled.

'Have nothing in your house that you do not know to be useful, or believe to be beautiful.'
WILLIAM MORRIS

Defining idea...

95

How did it go?

Q **I'm confused; I've been told that the eclectic look is very fashionable in interiors. How can I achieve that if I have to shove everything away into cupboards?**

A   *It's all a question of degree. The point of this chapter has not been to try to persuade you to live the life of an ascetic monk; if you have collections that you like to have around you that's fine. However, when it comes to putting your house on the market, you must have a strategy for quickly creating a look that will have universal appeal. You may love your collections of stuffed weasels but there is no guarantee that a prospective buyer will too.*

Q **Isn't renting a unit in a local storage facility rather an expensive way to de-clutter a house?**

A   *No, it is surprisingly cost effective – and possibly one of the best investments that you can make in a selling campaign. Banishing a large proportion of your possessions – even those that you use on a pretty regular basis – will create the feeling that a house is bigger than it really is. Also, even if you have a huge amount of storage, it never looks great when it is crammed with boxes and old clothes.*

22

Driving ambition

You'd be surprised at how much just one parking space can add to the value of a property.

Such is the demand for parking that a lock-up garage in a major city can sell for as much as a small house.

In towns – and even in some villages – parking has become an extremely precious commodity. The combination of more cars, higher density housing, short-sighted developers and stricter council controls means that it is one of the great property headaches of the twenty-first century.

You only need to look at the way that a typical Victorian residential street has developed since it was built, to realise the problems. The first most obvious difference is the advent of the motor car, and there might be one, two, if not three cars per household. In cases where a house has been split into a number of different units, the number of cars per building might rise to seven or eight. Add to that the rise in 'infill' development – in which new, smaller houses are built in the gardens of larger ones – and you have all the ingredients for an area that looks like one enormous traffic jam.

Here's an idea for you... **When planning off-street parking, the best hunting ground for inspiration lies in other people's solutions. However, the exercise should also teach you what doesn't work, so try to learn from mistakes as well as successes. The best place to look for good solutions is in areas where there is a lot of high value housing where architects might have been employed to find the best solution. Other people's ideas are there to be copied!**

The problem is particularly bad in areas where there are a large number of family houses – householders are often reluctant to sacrifice their gardens to create off street parking. Another black spot is where developers have created high density housing without investing in underground parking areas.

So that's the problem. What's the solution? Ideally, we'd all drive just one car or take to bicycles but the only sensible approach is to tackle the reality rather than the dream. While many local councils have created residents' parking areas that allow householders to park a limited number of vehicles on the street, there's no doubt that the ideal option is off-street parking, particularly for families that have to ferry shopping bags and small children to and from their house.

Depending on a property, there are four different types of parking option. The most common and space efficient is the 'in/out' parking space that allows room for parking just one or two cars with no room for manoeuvre (and is a nightmare on busy residential roads). Next is a larger version in which you can do an easy three point turn to turn your car around. Then there's the luxurious 'turning circle' drive that allows a car to sweep in and out of the drive without reversing and will accommodate a number of cars. For convenience, all of these are near either the front or the back door but in some cases a less desirable option is a 'remote drive' which is away from any of the entrance doors to the property.

In the absence of any parking, choosing which of these you want will involve weighing up issues of logistics and aesthetics. For example, there's little point in adding three parking spaces if it's going to involve turning the front of your house into something akin to an office car park. Also, if the size of the garden is limited, you may not want to sacrifice half of it in order to create a giant, sweeping 'turning circle' driveway.

The aim should be to create parking that is sympathetic to the surroundings – and the secret lies in realistic demands, great design and attractive materials.

If the project is quite complex, involving the reconfiguration of steps or walls, it is essential that you employ the services of an architect, part of whose job will be to help with any planning issues. The joy of architects, is that they are the masters of planning space and a good one will help you to incorporate a drive that sits happily in its environment.

'When Solomon said that there was a time and a place for everything he had not encountered the problem of parking his automobile.'
BOB EDWARDS

Defining
idea…

The materials you choose will also have a huge impact on the way that a drive looks. Here is an at-a-glance guide to the main options.

1   *Gravel.* A great option for flat 'turning circle drives' that also has the advantage of being loathed by burglars (it makes a distinctive 'crunching' noise when you walk on it). In small spaces it also has a habit of 'leaking' on to the road which can look messy.
2   *Block paving.* Looks very smart but in some cases it can also look quite municipal. Choose with care. Old fashioned equivalents such as granite sets can look better at period properties.
3   *Stone.* Expensive but pleasing. Beware of composite fakes – they never look great.
4   *Concrete.* At a push it can look good in contemporary surroundings but it often looks like a short cut.
5   *The car turntable.* This may be something of a desperate measure, but if space is so tight that you can only drive a car in, but not turn it round, the solution is a turntable that revolves so that your car faces the right direction. It is an expensive option but may solve severe parking difficulties.

THE VALUE OF EXTRA PARKING

Estate agents often try to put a value on an extra space but it is an inexact science. So much depends on local conditions. Nevertheless you should never underestimate the value of parking – particularly if, when you come to sell, your property is being compared with one that doesn't have parking. The issue has become so fraught that the chances are that your house could sell more quickly and for a higher price than a house with a higher specification.

How did it go?

Q **Although I don't use my front garden, I'm concerned that creating off-street parking will compromise the look of the front of my house.**

A *A combination of good design and high quality materials will help create a visually pleasing solution. Also, remember that all houses evolve to suit the changing needs of their owners; you will never get the most from your house if it is set in aspic.*

Q **Because my house is on a slope – and the garden quite small – I can only create parking that is a long way from the house. Is it still worth doing?**

A *Definitely, yes. The people that it might put off are families who have to ferry shopping and children a long distance, which is a tiresome business, particularly on a cold, wet, windy night. However, remote parking is still better than none at all.*

Q **What about the environmental impact of everyone turning their front garden into a parking area?**

A *This is something that you can factor in when planning any changes. Even the smallest of spaces can accommodate a tub or two for planting attractive flowers and shrubs; and larger frontages can include borders containing smart and easy to maintain plants.*

A treat for feet

As an alternative to radiators, heated floors might seem like a futuristic option but the Romans introduced them thousands of years ago.

And there's nothing so luxurious as the feel of the warmth radiating up through the soles of your feet.

Often it isn't the complex and expensive projects that will add the most value to a property but those that are the result of thought and planning. Potential purchasers might put their heads round the door of a new extension and nod in appreciation but minutes later be cooing over the beautiful worktops, hardwood floors or the lovely roll-top bath. One feature that falls into this category is underfloor heating, which offers so many benefits that it is a surprise that more people don't fit it. Underfloor heating is a system of electric cables or hot water pipes that lie beneath the surface of a floor. Most people are surprised to discover that it isn't a modern, hi tech phenomenon but actually a Roman invention – albeit in a slightly different guise – that was introduced to the chillier extremes of their empire, particularly Britain.

FIVE GOOD REASONS TO FIT UNDERFLOOR HEATING

1   It makes radiators redundant. Wave goodbye to ugly, bulky designs and interminable lengths of piping. Remember that as well as looking ugly, radiators also take up wall space and determine where you may be able to put furniture.
2   It provides a natural-feeling, even heat. Because the heat is gently radiated over a large area, rather than intensely just from a few radiators, it creates a much more diffuse, ambient atmosphere that heats your feet the most (mmmmh) and your head the least.
3   It is more energy efficient than a system of radiators. Estimates vary, but underfloor heating is significantly cheaper to run than conventional heating. However, remember that if it isn't fitted as part of a refurbishment project, it can be expensive to install.
4   It is far kinder to building materials and furnishings. The gentle, even heat created by an underfloor system is much less likely to damage or warp materials used in period buildings, particularly timber.
5   It is better for asthma sufferers. They will benefit from underfloor heating because it is less likely than a system of radiators to circulate dust mites.

Here's an idea for you...

To discover the impact that underfloor heating can have on a room draw a scale plan of the space that you have and consider how it would be transformed by the absence of radiators. The chances are that the layout of a room is governed by the position of your radiators, so consider how you would change the position of furniture.

WHERE YOU CAN USE UNDERFLOOR HEATING

There is a common misconception that underfloor heating can only be used in floors that have a capacity to conduct heat such as stone and terracotta. In fact, it can be fitted beneath almost any type of surface including carpet and wood. However, every different type of material will come with its own set of limitations and demands, and it is for this reason that it is essential that you use a contractor who is experienced in this sort of work.

GOING THE WHOLE HOG

In a new build house, a major refurbishment or conversion (i.e. of a chapel, barn or former industrial building) there will be far greater, more cost effective opportunities to create underfloor heating than in a partial refurbishment of an existing property. The result is not just an increase in energy efficiency but also a much simpler, more pared down interior.

CHERRY PICKING AREAS FOR UNDERFLOOR HEATING

If you're partially refurbishing a property here is a list of areas that should be on your wish list, in order of priority.

1   *Bathrooms.* There's no doubt that underfloor heating is a great luxury in bathrooms because of the comfort that it gives to feet. It is a particular asset in bathrooms where there is a 'cold' material on the floor such as stone or terracotta. Remember that when you fit underfloor heating, in the absence of a radiator you will still need a heated towel rail.
2   *Kitchens.* Because there is so much competition for wall space, underfloor heating is a real boon.
3   *Halls.* Large spaces such as halls and corridors will particularly benefit from the gentle, even heat of underfloor heating.

Defining idea…

'**May you have warmth in your igloo, oil in your lamp and peace in your heart.**'
Eskimo proverb

How did it go?

Q   Why is underfloor heating so expensive to install?

A   *It isn't so much that underfloor heating is expensive – it is simply that radiators are relatively cheap. Because underfloor heating is still regarded as quite a 'niche' product it is possible for contractors to charge a premium price for it. As demand grows, they will become more competitive and prices will fall.*

Q   Because it is so expensive to install, is it also very expensive to maintain?

A   *While it is expensive, underfloor heating is surprisingly simple, so there is far less chance of it going wrong than conventional heating systems. It is really no more complicated than an electric blanket. The reason that it is expensive to fit is because of the disruption that it causes, particularly the amount of work required to conceal it.*

Q   Is there any point in fitting underfloor heating in a space where there is a fuel burning range?

A   *You should fit underfloor heating anywhere that you have radiators. Most people fit radiators in kitchens to create an even heat with a number of heat sources – and because there might be times of year that they don't want a range on – i.e. the summer.*

24

The 2-in-1 room

In small properties multi-purpose rooms are often essential – and can help to add value.

But even in the biggest properties, there are rooms that will have to serve more than one purpose. Here is how to master the art of creating a multitasking room.

Inevitably, there will be properties that have enormous demands made on them. Period houses were designed in a different age, when children slept three to a bed, when the kitchen consisted of nothing but a simple stove and people were happy to bathe once a week in metal tub. And even when a period house is extended, the chances are that it won't provide all the space that modern life demands.

What is important to bear in mind is that a multi-purpose room should rely as little as possible on moving furniture around – a mark of success is to be able to use the same space for two different activities. There are two things that every successful multi-purpose room has in common – perfectly planned space and brilliant storage. The result will be two rooms that looks a natural in whichever role they are playing.

Here's an idea for you... **The only way to create a successful layout in a multi-purpose room is to try out as many different configurations as you can. In particular, you should try each variation for the different purposes that the room will serve. While you are deciding on the best layout, leave your experimental configurations in place for a few days, so that any possible problems become apparent.**

THE KITCHEN/DINING ROOM

This is the most popular doubling up of function – and in many senses, the easiest. The problem lies in the fact that the term kitchen/dining room is, in many senses a misnomer. Rooms that serve both these purposes tend to be for far more than just cooking and eating. In family homes they are often used as home offices, media rooms and living rooms, too.

Layout: Try to create well-defined areas, so it is obvious where one function stops and another starts. The ideal is a long rectangular room with a dining area at one end and kitchen at the other – if space allows, a freestanding 'island unit' workspace creates a natural barrier between one end and another. If the room is square try to create the area in a corner, with fitted bench seating if space is tight. If space is very tight consider a 'bar' arrangement that is either fitted to the wall or is an integral part of the cabinetry.

Storage: Because dining requires relatively few accessories that aren't already in a kitchen, storage is rarely a problem but consider fitted bench seating which provides useful space. Also ensure that any kitchen table you have is fitted with a drawer.

THE LIVING ROOM/DINING ROOM

Again, creating two different 'zones' is key. A good way to do this is with a console table that is placed behind a sofa, dividing a room and providing a useful place to place low lighting, such as table lamps. A low cabinet that provides storage and somewhere to serve food is also a useful ingredient.

GUEST BEDROOM/DRESSING ROOM

More often than not, there will be at least one bedroom in a house that is only used on an occasional basis and it makes sense to give it some other purpose, such as a dressing room. Fit plenty of sleek, fitted storage, so that when it is used as a guest bedroom, it will look calm and tidy.

THE LIVING ROOM/SPARE ROOM

When bedrooms are in short supply – or devoted to some other use – it is easy to create a living room that can quickly and easily be turned into a guest room with the help of a sofa bed. If so, try to provide storage for duvets and have an arrangement in which side tables can easily double as bedside tables.

THE 'VIRTUAL' HOME OFFICE

There was a time when there would have been a temptation to combine a bedroom or dining

'Just as we have two eyes and two feet, duality is part of life.'

CARLOS SANTANA

Defining idea...

room with a home office. However, with the leaps and bounds in technology it is now possible to use almost any room as a home office, as long as you have a laptop and a cupboard to store your filing, hard drive and a printer. That said, if you have room for a dedicated office where a potential buyer could imagine running a business, you may consider it to be good use of space.

THE 'VIRTUAL' PLAY ROOM

In many cases you won't have space to create a dedicated play room. However, on the whole, children are happy to play anywhere that there is a clear, comfortable surface, so the most important facility is a large, easily accessed, well organised cupboard where they can keep toys. Remember to 'edit' toys regularly by putting some away in longer term storage (i.e. in a garage) – partly to stave off boredom and partly to save space.

Q   **If space is at a premium, isn't it just better to consider building an extension?**   *How did it go?*

A   *It really depends on whether you'll get a sufficient return on you invest-ment. Of course, extensions can be a good way to enhance the value of a property – but multi-purpose rooms are another means of maximising value, too. Also, remember that there are some rooms – dining rooms and living rooms in particular – that will be under exploited if you don't find some other purpose for them.*

Q   **If I create too many multi-purpose rooms, isn't there a danger that the house might end up looking a bit of a mess?**

A   *The secret of a multi-purpose room is that it should look like any other – when it is used as a bedroom it should look like any other bedroom and when it is being used as a dressing room that is what it should look like. The secret to achieving this is with plenty of planning – and plenty of stor-age.*

Q   **So effectively you are getting two rooms for the price of one?**

A   *Yes, that's the idea.*

25

Big is beautiful

You can't devote too much space to a kitchen, even if it's at the expense of other rooms.

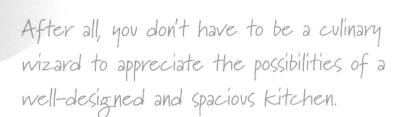

After all, you don't have to be a culinary wizard to appreciate the possibilities of a well-designed and spacious kitchen.

There are plenty of rooms – bedrooms and bathrooms being the most obvious examples – which can be radically minimalised without compromising their function. There are even some rooms, notably dining rooms and home offices that you could easily sacrifice altogether without a care in the world. But you'd need real courage to consider shrinking a kitchen by even a millimetre. The reason? Well there's no clever way of explaining the logic behind this; quite simply, punters are obsessed with the size of a kitchen.

Kitchens are now for far more than cooking – we eat in them, work in them, some of us even relax and watch television in them. And the more of these activities that we can do in comfort, the more attracted we are to the kitchen. It's as simple as that.

Here's an idea for you... **Create scale outlines of the key elements that you'd like to include in a kitchen. Include any floor mounted kitchen units, freestanding appliances, a kitchen table and an island unit. Rather than trying to fit them into a kitchen, arrange your ideal configuration and fit the kitchen around them.**

In many undeveloped properties, kitchens will barely be big enough to stand in, let alone play a pivotal role in family life. And there's no escaping the fact that in order to maximise the value of almost any property, it is essential that a kitchen is as large as space and budget will allow. The answer lies in some lateral thought.

FIVE WAYS TO EXPAND THE SIZE OF A KITCHEN

1 Join it to an adjacent room. Consider annexing any adjacent rooms such as pantries, outhouses or even reception rooms. You'd be surprised how inexpensive this can be – and there are plenty of rooms that can be sacrificed.
2 Build an extension. If the house is in a terrace, don't just consider pushing out backwards – you can also widen the space by extending into the side return (this also has the advantage of not eating into the garden). A side extension with a glass roof will create a wonderful, light-filled space.
3 Add a conservatory. This can offer a relatively inexpensive way to add space and light. The classic layout involves extending to the back of the house in order to create an eating area.

4 Move it to a bigger room. If you have a small, poky kitchen but a larger living room you could consider reversing the roles. There are two variations to this plan; one is to simply swap one for the other, creating a big kitchen and small living room, which in many cases is a good trade. Alternatively, if you have a classic Victorian 'double ended' living room, you could consider moving the kitchen to one end creating one large open plan space that serves both purposes.

5 Cheat. There will be occasions when you can't extend a kitchen – or don't consider doing so to be a good investment. In this case, you need some careful planning. In order that the room looks and feels bigger, try to minimise the amount of fitted units and appliances. Could you free up cupboard space by hanging pots and pans from hooks attached to a wall? Could you stack the fridge over the dishwasher? Even if you don't create enough space for a dining area, you will make the room feel less claustrophobic.

FILLING THE SPACE

■ So, once you've created a bigger kitchen, what do you do with it? The single most important element has to be a table. If there isn't room for a table there are two space saving options: if space really is tight, you could consider a wall-mounted bar, or a wall-mounted table that folds out. Another good use of space is a bench seat fitted into the corner of the room which creates space-efficient seating.

■ You could also consider an 'island unit' that creates a great place to prepare food – it can include a sink, cooker and storage.

'The need for expansion is as genuine an instinct in man as the need in a plant for the light.'

MATTHEW ARNOLD

Defining idea...

115

Q   Are kitchens as important in a small one bedroom property as in a large family house?

A   *No, not as important. However, if you really can't increase the size of a kitchen in a small property, it is much more important that you ensure it is near the area that you eat. If possible, consider creating an open plan area that provides for eating, cooking and dining.*

Q   If the property is unlikely to be used as a family home, is it still necessary to put so much effort into creating a large kitchen?

A   *Yes, even couples and those living on their own will value a large kitchen. Also, remember that potential purchasers don't just buy properties with their own needs in mind; many will also be buying as an investment.*

Q   What about using small items of furniture such as stools and folding tables for making a kitchen look bigger?

A   *For some mysterious reason, large items of furniture often make small rooms look bigger than scaled down furniture. Also, people have an amazing capacity to notice that furniture is scaled down and it can accentuate the problem.*

26

The light fantastic

Adding glass doors and roof lights can completely transform a variety of spaces from kitchen to dark stairwells.

Banishing the gloom from your home not only looks good, it has health benefits too.

Natural light is one of the most important but most often forgotten elements in an interior design. Frequently, we simply take it for granted and only really notice it when it is absent. Worse still, because it's such an intangible element, few of us know how to make the most of it.

When viewing a property, it is essential that you visit at different times of day to see how the light changes as the sun moves through the sky. If owners leave lights on in the middle of the day, they might be trying to mask a problem. Nevertheless, there are plenty of ways to tackle the problem – and it isn't necessarily a reason not to buy a house. Here are some key light-related subjects to consider when you're planning to decorate or refurbish a property.

1   *Windows.*
    - Where possible, look for opportunities where you can add windows – or make existing ones larger.
    - Make sure that the windows aren't obscured with curtains – if you have curtains make sure that they can be pulled well back.
    - When they aren't in use, roman and roller blinds are more compact than curtains with the result that they allow more light through a window.

2   *Sky lights.* Fit these wherever possible – in both single storey extensions and in the top floor of a building. There are few better ways to transform a room – and have the advantage of creating plenty of light while maintaining privacy which is ideal in bedrooms or when a room overlooks a brick wall or busy road. They are also a great option for the ceilings of halls and stairwells.

3   *Walls.* One of the advantages of removing internal walls is that they maximise the amount of light in a property. Also, if building an extension, consider replacing a wall with a floor-to-ceiling window.

4   *Doors.* External and internal doors fitted with glass panels help to maximise light. In modern properties or extensions try to fit doors that are completely made of glass. Many architects fit folding doors that run the whole width of a building.

5   *Paint colours, furniture and flooring.* When decorating the walls of a house there is a great deal that you can do to maximise the amount of light. Pale paint colours, flooring and upholstery will all help to reflect light and create an airy feel.

6   *Mirrors.* An important – but too often forgotten – weapon in the war against gloom is the humble mirror. Covering an entire wall with mirror might sound like a radical move but it can transform a dark room and can be surprisingly unobtrusive. In fact, it can help to make the room seem more spacious too. Also, whenever possible, try to place mirrors strategically opposite windows.

7 *Conservatories.* One good way to inject huge amounts of light into a dark house is with a conservatory. Adding one to a kitchen not only adds significantly to the space, it also opens up the whole area to the outside, transforming even cold, north-facing rooms.

8 *Trees.* This might sound obvious – but you'd be surprised how often this issue is ignored – shrubs and trees can play big part in shrouding an interior from natural light, particularly in the summer. Where possible, remove any plants that are caus- ing a light obstruction – light interiors are far more important than a treasured wisteria.

9 *Too much light.* You can overdo it of course. Too much glass doesn't just cause prob- lems in excessive heat and lack of privacy – it can also create a painful glare on sunny days (it's not unusual to see the inhabitants of modern glass buildings wearing sunglasses inside – and not as a fashion statement).

Paint plays a key part in creating a light, airy interior. If planning to paint a room, don't just consider whether a colour fits in with your scheme; also consider its capacity to reflect light (these two qualities won't necessarily be the same thing). Paint patches of any of the samples that you are considering on a wall and study their reflective qualities at different times of day.

Here's an idea for you...

'Space and light and order. Those are things that men need just as much as they need bread or a place to sleep.'

LE CORBUSIER

Defining idea...

119

How did it go?

Q **Isn't the cheapest, simplest solution to the problem of a dark interior to have plenty of artificial light and pale paintwork?**

A *If there are really no ways to maximise the sources of natural light in a property, then these are your only options. But don't kid yourself that artificial light is a substitute for the real thing – plenty of natural light doesn't just make a room look better, it also make its occupants feel better. However, if you are simply 'turning over' a property for a quick sale, you might decide that there is no point in undertaking huge amounts of expensive structural work.*

Q **Are there any artificial lights that mimic daylight better than others?**

A *Yes, low voltage spots create a more even, purer light than conventional light bulbs. Try to avoid the institutional glow of strip lighting at all costs.*

Q **Won't increasing the size of windows have a negative impact on the appearance of a property?**

A *Good question. You have to take particular care when increasing the size of windows in a period property and check with your local planning department. This is an issue that a good architect will help with.*

Q **Isn't air conditioning the answer to the problem of heat created by conservatories and large windows?**

A *No, not really. It's expensive, noisy and ecologically unsound. It should only be used in extremis.*

27

The dream dressing room

A dedicated room for storing clothes and getting dressed isn't just a luxury – it's also a smart way to add value to your bedroom.

Dressing rooms may once have been the preserve of mansion dwellers, but now everyone can experience the good life.

There are two convincing reasons for creating a dressing room: the first is that it will add significantly to the quality of your daily life; the other is that it will have a magical knock-on effect in your bedroom, ridding it of the tyranny of cupboards, clothes, jackets, trousers and a dressing table.

There are several different options to consider.

1   *The en suite dressing room.* If space allows, this is an ideal scenario – an adjacent space that is seamlessly joined to a bedroom offering a wide range of storage, preferably fitted, plus a chest of drawers.
2   *The walk-in wardrobe.* This is a small but perfectly formed space which is a variation of the en suite dressing room and offers storage and possibly just enough space to get dressed in.
3   *The 'His and Hers' dressing room/walk-in wardrobe.* If space allows, this is a great luxury that enables a couple each to have their own dedicated space.

Here's an idea for you... **When planning a walk-in wardrobe try to accommodate only those clothes that you use on a regular basis. You'll be amazed at the disparity between these clothes and those that you currently keep in your cupboard. I'm not suggesting that you take them all to a charity shop – simply that you put them into long term storage. Editing down the amount of clothes you keep close to hand will have a positive impact on anywhere that you plan to keep clothes.**

4   *The 'remote' dressing room.* If the layout of a property doesn't allow you to create an en suite dressing room, you can dedicate a nearby room to the purpose. While this isn't an ideal arrangement it nevertheless offers the same benefits.

5   *The bathroom/dressing room.* With careful planning it is possible to create a room that combines both these functions – if space is tight you could consider fitting a shower rather than a bath.

6   *The spare bedroom/dressing room.* If you have plenty of good fitted storage, there is no reason why you shouldn't combine both functions in one room. The objective should be that when the room is being used as a bedroom, there shouldn't be any obvious signs of its alter ego. The last thing you want is for guests to have to wade through piles of discarded clothes.

STORAGE AND LIGHTING

Fitted storage is ideal because it makes the best use of space. The interior should offer plenty of good storage systems including hanging space, shelves for folded items such as jerseys and shirts plus pigeonhole storage

for shoes. You'll need a space for large items such as hat boxes and possibly items of luggage, and you may want to consider creating storage for small items such as jewellery.

Good light is essential in both cupboard space and in the space where you'll be getting dressed. Low voltage spot lights are ideal. If possible, natural light will also offer huge benefits.

JUSTIFYING THE SPACE

Like a laundry room, utility room or a media room, a dressing room is something of a luxury. As such, it is one of those options that you'll have to weigh up when planning space. However, it's worth remembering that if you have a room dedicated to storage it means that you can have a much smaller bedroom; the only essential ingredients in a bedroom are a bed and a bedside light. If you can find the space, however, it won't just offer enormous benefits to you – it will also alter the perception of the property.

CREATING A DRESSING ROOM OUT OF NOTHING

Many interior designers consider that, for most homes, a big bedroom has minimal value. This is certainly true in that, with plenty of space to spare, a large bedroom is an agreeable – if somewhat superfluous – luxury. But in the majority of cases, a big bedroom is an opportunity to do something much more interesting, such as carve up the space to create either a dressing room or a bathroom – or preferably both. The secret lies in dividing the space so that it creates harmonious, well furnished rooms.

'I like my money right where I can see it ... hanging in my closet.'

SARAH JESSICA PARKER

Defining idea...

123

Q   Are you saying that a bedroom will be severely compromised if I don't have a walk-in wardrobe or a separate dressing room?

A   *No, no, no! Both these things are luxuries rather than essentials. There will be plenty of properties where it would be impossible to create either. However, in the absence of a walk-in wardrobe or dressing room it is essential that clothes storage is kept under control. If there isn't enough room in a bedroom, move some clothes elsewhere.*

Q   Is a dressing room more important than a bedroom?

A   *So much depends on the property. In a six bedroom property it might be a sacrifice that you can safely make. Even in a small property that is unlikely to ever be used as a family home, it is possible to justify a dressing room, particularly if it takes the pressure off other rooms.*

Q   What about splitting a second bedroom?

A   *This is a great idea if you can create two functional rooms. However, it might be cheaper and more convenient simply to create a dual purpose room instead.*

28

Sofa so good

The upholstered furniture you choose can show a room off to its best advantage.

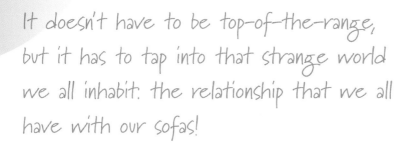

It doesn't have to be top-of-the-range, but it has to tap into that strange world we all inhabit: the relationship that we all have with our sofas!

Too often, home owners who are refurbishing houses to sell get so wound up in the structure of a building that they run out of steam by the time that they get to the stage at which they have to start filling it with those essentials such as furniture. It is perhaps because it is so straightforward ('Well, you just go to a shop don't you?') that it is treated as an afterthought. In fact, there's a very high risk that if you don't get the furniture right, you might as well not have bothered to spend all that time, effort – oh, and thousands of pounds – in the first place. By now – particularly if you're an architect – you'll think that I'm exaggerating. And if you're an architect you'll consider me shallow, frivolous and lacking in depth.

And you'd be right – but these are qualities that I share with the vast majority of people who may be thinking of buying your property. Yes, you might have lavished

Here's an idea for you... **When trying to decide on the right sofa, try to collect together as many images as you can from a wide range of different sources (magazines, brochures, the internet). If creating a new scheme, cut out pictures of those that you are considering and create a collage – or mood board – that includes examples of other elements such as fabric samples and flooring. It will help you to work out whether the sofa will look right in the environment that you are planning.**

insane amounts of love and attention on creating beautiful light-filled spaces, fabulous finishes, and exquisite architectural detail. But what their eye will be drawn to, if they are sharing the space with a hideous sofa covered in fabric that looks like woolly hosiery, is that rather than the architectural beauty that you have created.

What you must bear in mind is that potential buyers will forgive you all sorts of sins – a dodgy dining room table, bad lighting and bumpy beds – but they will never, ever let you get away with a sofa that doesn't fit in with its environment. The fact is that we all have quite intimate relationships with our sofas; after our beds, they are the items of furniture on which most of us spend the most time. The result is that even the most design illiterate buyer will

have a view on which type of sofa will fit which type of room. And the result is that you get it wrong at your peril.

Here is an at-a-glance guide to choosing the right sofa for the right interior.

- *Contemporary-style urban property.* Depending on space and budget, go for something with clean simple lines in a pale colour. If space allows, consider an L shaped sofa that makes a great statement. Try to avoid anything too James Bond, as the futuristic look will turn off those with a taste for simple classic furniture and they will find it hard to stomach.
- *Contemporary-style country property.* Similar to the above but simpler and softer in shape. Choose fabrics with rough textures such as linen or felt in a natural colour.
- *Classic town house.* The ideal shape would be a club style sofa and chairs in a plain velvet, linen or leather.
- *Classic country house.* Similar to the above but you may want to consider a fabric in a muted pattern such as a bold floral or stripe. Alternatively you could opt for a Chesterfield in any of the above fabrics.
- *Classic country cottage.* Space will be the key deciding factor here; the ideal choice might be a small, simple Victorian-style sofa with clean lines in a plain or simple, cottagey floral.

> **'Style is primarily a matter of instinct.'**
> BILL BLASS

Defining idea...

SIZE

Sofas are the exception to the rule that large items of furniture make a small room seem bigger. Never fill a small – or even a medium-sized room with a large sofa unless it is for nothing other than watching television.

QUALITY

Choose the quality of a sofa according to your budget. Very expensive upholstered furniture won't be a make or break feature of a house – it is more important that it is the right style and size and is upholstered in appropriate fabric. For mid-to-upmarket properties, a middle of the range sofa is fine. For modest properties it doesn't matter if it's cheap – it is more important that it is good looking and clean.

SOFAS IN KITCHENS AND BEDROOMS

If space allows, a sofa in either of these rooms is a good move, partly because it looks so luxurious – and partly because it emphasises that a room has plenty of spare space.

Q **So are you suggesting that expensive sofas are a waste of money?**

How did it go?

A *No, not all. There is no greater pleasure than relaxing on a beautifully made sofa. The point I am making is that if you are decorating a house with the specific, short term objective of selling it, then there isn't much point in splashing out on a top-of-the-range sofa. You should only buy one if it suits your own purposes. The joy of a good sofa is a very private pleasure – few people will look long and hard enough to realise its attractions. Also remember that any potential buyer will be aware that you won't be leaving the sofas behind. The important rule is that you don't have a sofa that will detract from the rest of the property.*

Q **But cheap ones are just as good?**

A *To the untrained eye a cheap sofa can look impressive. However, they aren't a great long term investment. Nevertheless they are infinitely preferable to an expensive but grubby sofa that has seen better days.*

Q **What about second-hand?**

A *It is worth considering second-hand but bear in mind that there is a high chance that you will have to have them re-upholstered, which can cost almost as much as buying a new, basic model. You can buy ready-made covers for some shapes.*

29

Why the beauty is in the details

Often it's the little touches that potential purchasers notice, from the house number to your kitchen door handles.

And with such a profusion of choice it's easy to get overwhelmed by the minutiae.

Ask a builder to buy you a light switch and you'll get the DIY shed standard. It won't be beautiful but then it won't be ugly either. It will be neither cheap nor expensive. High quality or low. It will just be the light switch equivalent of beige. The same will be true with almost any other item that builders choose, from guttering and paving slaps to taps and ceiling roses. This is not a tirade against builders, it's simply an unwritten rule that unless you specify exactly what you want, you'll simply get something that combines price and functionality.

The way to raise the game rarely involves a great deal more money – it simply requires much more time spent researching the alternatives. Often they are right there under your nose. Or sometimes, they might require a bit of a hunting game – a quest that will take you to some specialist supplier out there in cyberspace.

Here's an idea for you...

If you want to see the difference that good detailing can make on the overall appearance of a property, visit a few luxury hotels. You don't have to stay, just go for a drink or for tea. While you are there make sure you examine every last detail; it won't just give you ideas, it will also demonstrate that it can be worth pushing the boat out when you're fitting out your own property. Creating the look and feel of luxury isn't necessarily about throwing money around – more often than not it is the result of plenty of thought and planning. What's more you're bound to enjoy the investigative experience!

Let's take garden paving slabs. Ask a builder to supply some and you'll get a grey, featureless piece of composite material that is quick and easy to lay. Job done. Bish bosh. Yet garden paving covers a huge breadth of options, in all sorts of different shapes, sizes, colours and materials. Go to a specialist supplier and you'll see that for a little extra – and a mere fraction of the total cost of the job, you can get something that looks like a million dollars.

This is just one example and you can never consider a decision made until you have seen every different variation on offer. The starting point of any search should be an internet trawl that will give you an idea of the scope of what's on offer.

THE TOP TEN HIGH PROFILE DETAILS

1   Ceramic tiles. There is more to tiles than the stark white squares you get find in public lavatories and abattoirs. Even if you can afford tiles with a wonderful hand made texture, consider a colour. Mosaic tiles can completely transform a room and, surprisingly, they are cheaper and easier to fit than they look.

2   *Bricks and paving.* Bricks that are deliberately made to look old are significantly more expensive than standard issue. However, for small quantities, the impact can far outweigh the investment. When looking at paving, small block paving often creates a look that is much more sympathetic to period buildings. Machine stone is better suited to urban house than riven stone which looks more rustic. When specifying *always* ask for a wide range of colours and prices.

3   *Doors.* Doors are such an important part of a house that it is essential that you consider investing in a model that looks good and doesn't feel too flimsy.

4   *Door numbers.* Simple slate is the most discreet option. Avoid anything tricksy; particularly the large 'statement' numbers favoured by contemporary architects.

5   *Door furniture.* Like internal door handles, we have such intimate, day-to-day contact with door furniture that it pays to push the boat out, even if the costs seem exorbitant when compared to the standard. On a black glossy door shiny nickel can look extremely smart.

6   *Glass.* There are handmade alternatives to modern, industrially made glass. Consider cylinder glass that has an uneven surface that makes it much more suitable for period buildings. Also consider etched glass in glazed doors and bathroom windows.

7   *Handles.* Good quality, functional door handles are essential. Brass feels most pleasant to touch but also consider more contemporary alternatives.

8   *Light switches.* Rather than standard white plastic, consider brushed steel or nickel, the slick good looks of which will more than justify the outlay. Another option is perspex that allows the paint or wallpaper beneath to be seen.

'God is in the details.'
LUDWIG MIES VAN DER ROHE

Defining
idea...

9   *Light flex.* Coloured or fabric covered flex looks so much better than white.
10   *Masonry paint.* Always look at alternatives to white because white can look
      austere, particularly in harsh sunlight. Stone colours often create a the smartest
      look.

How did it go?

Q   I assume that all this attention to detail is only worthwhile if one is renovating a high value property?

A   No, no, no, not at all. Imagine the scenario of a purchaser who is down-shifting from a large luxury house to a terraced cottage; there is a high chance that good detailing will do an enormous amount to change their perceptions of the property. Often these things are subliminal but nevertheless extremely powerful.

Q   Are there any exceptions at the bottom end of the market?

A   Yes. Properties that are likely to be bought by buy-to-let landlords are unlikely to benefit from any niceties. A combination of functionality and cost are much more powerful factors.

30

Digging for gold

**There may be untapped potential beneath your house –
but excavate with care.**

*You'll need more skills than a mole or a
badger to create a brilliant basement.*

One of the most remarkable achievements of the home improvement industry
in the last decade is the extent to which it has succeeded in eking out every last
inch of space from a property – not just within existing structures but in upwards
and outwards expansion. What the domestic architecture of the early twenty-first
century will be remembered for won't be architectural style but logistical ingenu-
ity. But surely most extraordinary of all is the change in the construction industry
– the creation of a new breed of builder-cum-mining engineer. The reason for this is
the discovery that almost as much as 25 per cent more floor area can be added to a
house by digging into the ground around its foundations.

Victorian house builders understood this concept well – they were masters of creating subterranean space that also served as habitable living areas. These weren't just
dark damp cellars; many were proper full height rooms. The classic Victorian town
house has a basement floor with one light filled room to the front and an array of
rooms behind, many of which didn't offer light.

While the idea seems good on paper, with a few exceptions the concept can be
flawed on a number of levels. As you'd imagine, excavating for space is a feat of

Here's an idea for you... **The only way to fully understand the implications of converting and extending a basement is to explore some completed projects – photographs simply aren't enough. Talk to a basement conversion specialist and ask if there are any projects that you could see. The most important factor to consider is the light – or lack of it.**

engineering that requires huge upheaval to the immediate surroundings; the existing structure has to be stabilised, the earth has to be removed, and the new living area made watertight (making underground accommodation watertight has been described as creating an 'inside out swimming pool.') In addition, the space will need all the services – water, drainage and electricity. Yet in all the excitement over the technical feat that this sort of building work requires it's easy to overlook the end result – that what it creates is not light, airy rooms but a dark, subterranean gloom that feels like a five star air raid shelter.

The place where excavating for space tends to work best is in very expensive high density areas where adding just one room will repay the massive investment that this sort of project requires. Yet, if you look at the sort of applications that the accommodation is used for, it tends to be limited to those that don't require natural light such as gyms, swimming pools and home cinemas – i.e. not essential living accommodation.

Yet these high profile projects that tend to generate a huge amount of publicity are just part of the story. There are plenty of less ambitious ways to add to space below ground level, such as extending out into light wells. However, even the more modest projects are expensive, relative to conventional back and roof extensions. When considering work of this type, it is essential that you find an architect, builder and surveyor who are experienced in this type of work.

GOOD USES FOR A CONVERTED BASEMENT

- Utility rooms
- Bathrooms
- Guest rooms
- An open plan kitchen (on condition that there are sufficient sources of natural light)
- A gym or swimming pool
- A dining room (or at least a dining room that you'll use at night)

BAD USES FOR A CONVERTED BASEMENT

- A living room
- A home office
- A bedroom that is in constant use.

'Think not about your frustrations, but about your unfulfilled potential.'
POPE JOHN XXIII

Defining idea...

TO DIG OR NOT TO DIG?

The starting point of the decision-making process must be an estimate of the cost. With this in mind, ask yourself the following questions.

- How does the cost compare with any other extension project that hasn't yet been carried out, such as a roof extension?
- How does the cost compare with cost of selling the house and moving somewhere bigger?
- Even if these costs are cheaper, will the space be compromised by the fact that it is below ground?
- Could you cope with the stress of such a major project?

- If the space is going to be used for a home gym or a wine cellar, do you live in an area where there is a market for these features?
- If a large proportion of the space is going to be used for storage, is this really a worthwhile use for it?

How did it go?

Q **In the 'To Dig Or Not To Dig' section, your line of questioning appears to suggest that you are of the 'Not To Dig' school. Are you really against it?**

A *In many cases, a straightforward conversion of a basement is likely to be a worthwhile project. My concern, however, is that increasingly people are considering ambitious projects that might not offer all the benefits that they imagine. It is one of those plans about which you should think long and hard before undertaking.*

Q **Given the choice between a major basement conversion or an extension, which would you choose?**

A *On the basis that the costs were the same, I'd go for the extension, even if it meant eating into the garden. A good extension creates plenty of light and lateral space. In an ideal world I would combine it with a simple basement conversion to create a utility room and storage.*

31

Not just for granny

Creating independent living accommodation isn't just useful for elderly relatives – it can be also be a useful source of extra income.

And if you decide to move on, your investment will make an attractive prospect for potential buyers.

Even in this world of high density development, there are still properties that offer surplus accommodation. After all, there is only so much space that you need for bedrooms, home offices, play rooms and storage – and if you have all these and there's still room to spare, it makes sense to put it to good use.

In some cases, you might be tempted to 'parcel up' the space and sell it off as separate accommodation but this creates problems all of its own such as issues over privacy, access and parking. The other problem is that once you've sold it off, it's gone for ever. Worse still, is the possibility that after tax, any initial gain will be dwarfed by the amount that your own property has lost. The joy of hanging on to separate accommodation is that you maintain privacy and you have an adaptable resource that may also provide an additional source of income.

WHERE TO LOOK FOR ACCOMMODATION

1   *Outbuildings.* Many properties – particularly those in rural areas – have former agricultural buildings that offer the perfect opportunity to create independent accommodation. However, there is no doubt that making them habitable is an expensive business, although creating a source of extra income with a long term let or bed and breakfast may help to offset the cost.

2   *Raised ground floor basements.* This is by far the most cost effective option – and also the most flexible, allowing you to create space that can either be independent or part of the main house. Remember, however, that you should try to insulate the space from the sound of the main house (the sound of footfall on wooden floors can drive those below insane).

3   *Extensions.* Raising the height of an extension to two storeys is not just a relatively inexpensive project but it also creates the opportunity for separate accommodation with its own independent access. With existing double height extensions you might also consider creating separate access. Alternatively, if you have a sufficiently large plot, you might want to consider a new double height extension.

Here's an idea for you... **Contact a number of local estate agents and ask them how much you might get for any separate accommodation that you might create. Also, go and view any accommodation that is on the market. It is also worth asking local home owners who let out bed and breakfast accommodation if you can see their accommodation.**

4   *New builds.* The cost of a new build is surprisingly inexpensive – and even if you don't want to sell it off immediately you would have the option to do so at a later date.

5   *Roof extensions.* While roof extensions offer a good way to create independent accommodation, access is likely to be a problem. The best use of an attic flat is as bed and breakfast accommodation.

POINTS TO CONSIDER

- When planning any project that will create independent rentable accommodation, the figure in the forefront of your mind must always be the net profit that it will yield.
- Ask a letting agent for an estimate of the rent your secondary property might yield – and how much demand there might be for this type of accommodation.
- You should also subtract tax, maintenance and letting fees from the rent you are quoted (remember that some of the cost incurred may be tax deductible).
- If you are considering letting part of a property you should create independent services such as heating and electricity.

THINKING LATERALLY ABOUT SEPARATE ACCOMMODATION

If planning separate accommodation it is important that you try to create in-built flexibility into the arrangement. For example, it can be useful to have accommodation that can easily be annexed to the house in the event that you need additional space for yourself, should you need it. Also, there are plenty of different ways in which you can use the same accommodation; for example, if you live in an area that is popular with holiday makers, you could consider either a long term let, a holiday let or bed and breakfast accommodation.

Reality check

Before taking the plunge you must consider the impact that letting out property will have on your daily life. Ask yourself the following questions.

'Independence is happiness.'
SUSAN B ANTHONY

Defining idea...

141

- Do I want strangers living in such close proximity?
- Will it compromise the privacy that I currently have?
- Is there enough car parking … and would I want to share it with tenants and their guests?
- Could the accommodation ever be soundproof?

How did it go?

Q Is it possible to finance a separate rental property with a buy-to-let mortgage?

A *Yes, depending on how much equity you have in the main property there is a chance that a bank or building society would lend you the money to develop a separate property.*

Q Is there any danger that I might devalue a property by creating separate accommodation?

A *No, not if you keep your wits about you. As long a there is sufficient flexibility to allow the use to be changed to suit a potential buyer's purposes, there shouldn't be a problem.*

Q But will it be considered a benefit?

A *Yes. Even if someone has no intention of letting accommodation out, they'll like the idea that they could. There are also sorts of other ways that separate accommodation can be used such as guest accommodation or for staff. And, of course, as a granny flat.*

Table matters

It may seem like an indulgence but if you have the space, a dedicated dining room can be a huge asset.

Formal eating at home may be far less popular now, but most of us still dream of being the perfect host or hostess.

It's almost a decade since style pundits predicted the death of the dining room. Their gloomy prognosis was that the dining room was nothing more than an anachronism, a hangover from the Victorian age when large houses had a retinue of staff to ferry food around the house. The future, they believed, lay in enormous kitchens that offered copious space not just for food preparation, but also eating, entertaining and relaxing. In many respects, their predictions have been spot on; in a lot of cases, dining rooms have been sacrificed to create bigger kitchens or to make larger living rooms, home offices and play rooms.

But like any other fashion, this one has been cyclical. In larger homes – or those where there aren't so many demands on space, people are rediscovering the luxury of a space that is purely for eating and entertaining. The look is also much more glamorous than before; gone is the fashion for decorating the dining rooms of nine-

Here's an idea for you... **Hotels offer some of the best examples of well-designed dining space. Surf the websites of smart, design-led hotels looking at photographs of their main dining rooms, and more importantly, their private dining rooms.**

teenth century house in deep reds that were typical of that period. Today the look is much more contemporary, influenced by the sleek interiors of hotels and restaurants.

Yet, in their new incarnation, most dining rooms offer greater flexibility than ever before; some serve as part time home offices, play rooms or libraries. Hand-in-hand with this new fashion is a more open-plan layout and seamless joins with living rooms, kitchens and hallways.

WEIGHING UP THE OPTIONS

There's no doubt that when selling a house, a dining room won't be valued as highly as other rooms, such as a large kitchen, living room or an en suite bedroom. Yet with careful planning it can also offer a useful, flexible space that can do much to add to the 'wow factor' of a room.

1   *Self-contained dining room versus kitchen dining room.* There's no doubt that there are huge advantages to eating in a self-contained, glamorous space that is removed from the clutter and chaos of the kitchen. However, remember that there are disadvantages, too. Food may have to be transferred a long distance from the kitchen and then served. There's also no doubt that eating in a kitchen or a kitchen–dining room can have a much more intimate feel than eating in a dining room – and it allows you to talk to your guests while doing last minute preparations and serving. Ultimately you may decide to get the best of both worlds by creating a dining room that is adjacent to the kitchen –

offering you the benefits of a self-contained dining room *and* a kitchen–dining room.

2   *Classic dining room ingredients.* Although it is tempting to create a rigid, period feel in Victorian and Georgian houses, try to create a traditional look that has a softer, more contemporary feel. While the historic look can be stunning it is an acquired taste and it is safer to plan a scheme with more universal appeal. Traditional dining furniture, paintings and accessories mix surprisingly well with fresh modern colours and contemporary looking finishes and materials. If you're choosing very traditional style curtain treatments, opt for plain rather than patterned fabric. For practicality, hard flooring such as wood or limestone works well. Natural flooring such as sisal or seagrass is a cheaper option.

3   *Contemporary dining room ingredients.* If choosing a contemporary look, remember that it needs to be both comfortable and glamorous – austere minimalism is rarely a winner. Combine a contemporary table with sleek, modern, comfortable chairs. For curtains, choose plain fabrics (anything lustrous such as silk, satin or Trevira works well) with a contemporary rivet heading or simple square pelmets. If choosing between blinds and curtains, remember that curtains have the advantage of absorbing sound which is important in sleek, contemporary interiors. Metallic wallpapers are perfect for this look – alternatively, lighting offers a good way to add interest to plain walls.

STORAGE

The chances are that there will be a great deal of 'dead space' in a dining room. Consider fitting deep alcoves with unobtrusive cupboards and shallow spaces with bookshelves. Anything that will take pressure off the rest of the house will help you to justify that space.

'After a good dinner one can forgive anybody, even one's own relations.'
OSCAR WILDE

Defining idea...

145

How did it go?

Q **The suggestions that you make for both classic and contem-porary dining rooms sound rather bland. What do I do with my grandfather's large collection of tribal spears and hunting prints?**

A *If you are planning to sell the property in the near future, you should put them into storage. Apart from anything else, they might put your guests off their food.*

Q **Is a period look really that much of a turn off?**

A *Not necessarily – but to a new generation of buyers it might well be. If you're going for a period feel it is better to create one that will appeal to a wide range of potential buyers.*

Q **But even if I have scope for a dining room, is there really any point in devoting so much space to a room that I'll only use occa-sionally?**

A *This isn't just about you. If you are developing a large, prestigious prop-erty and there is space for a dining room, you should definitely consider creating one. Even if you don't use it for entertaining, you could use it as a home office.*

Hit the deck

A deck is perfect for some types of garden – but incongruous in others.

So how do you decide between a traditional lawn and a chic wooden wonder?

One of the most significant ways in which homes have changed in the last decade or so, is the way that increasingly there is a seamless join between the inside and outside. There are two key elements that have helped to precipitate this evolution – one is the growth in popularity of the conservatory, which blurs the boundaries between the garden and the interior of the house. The other is the growth of the wooden deck – the early twenty-first century version of the patio – which offers an easy way to create a continuation of an indoor floor in the garden.

FIVE GOOD REASONS WHY YOU MIGHT WANT A DECK

1 Decks are cheaper and easier to construct than a patio.
2 They also have a more relaxed feel that is warmer and softer underfoot than crazy paving. They particularly appeal to anyone who loves the southern hemisphere where they have been popular for centuries.

3   Because they are made of wood they are lighter and more versatile, offering easier ways to create different levels without hugely complicated building work.
4   Because they are so light they are ideal for roof terraces.
5   In small urban gardens they offer a low maintenance alternative to grass.

FIVE GOOD REASONS YOU MAY NOT WANT A DECK

1   Whatever the cost advantages they offer, they will never last as long as stone, concrete or terracotta.
2   When decks are wet, they can become slippery.
3   A deck requires maintenance.
4   If you drop charcoal on a deck it will burn.
5   It might well be a fad – and the chances are that not only will it look a tired in a few years' time – but also rather dated.

Here's an idea for you...

Draw a scale plan of the area where you are considering fitting a deck and try to plan as many different configurations as you can. Because it is relatively easy to create different levels, the possibilities are almost endless. Once you have looked at all the different options you should then discuss them with the builder who is going to carry out the work.

TO DECK OR NOT TO DECK?

Yet the question of whether or not you should fit a deck has less to do with weighing up the pros and cons and more to do with the type and style of property that you are refurbishing. For example, in a traditionally decorated period house in the country there is a chance that the slightly exotic look of a deck will seem somewhat out of place. Alternatively, in the garden of a sleek contemporary home it can look perfectly in keeping with its surroundings.

A deck is also one of those relatively inexpensive elements that can completely change the perception of a property. For example, given the choice between two small, virtually identical flats, most younger buyers would be drawn to one with a sleek deck, rather than a muddy, high maintenance patch of earth planted with a few token shrubs. And when space is at a premium, a deck also has the advantage of feeling like an extension of indoor space – particularly when entertaining in the summer.

THE DECK AS AN 'OUTDOOR ROOM'

If you're considering installing a deck, bear in mind that it won't just benefit your garden – it will also have a significant impact on the inside of the property. Decks can be used to create an 'outdoor room' that will give you a great deal more entertaining space during the summer. With this in mind, treat the space like you would any other room; buy comfortable furniture, lighting and accessories. Because decks have a cool, contemporary feel, it makes sense to furnish them with cool contemporary furniture. Sleek, steel tables with benches rather than chairs are the obvious choice.

REMOTE DECKS

Remember that decks don't have to adjoin the property. In large gardens you can create areas of deck away from the house that will offer a great place for outdoor entertaining. You might also want to consider constructing a deck around a summer house.

'You have to have a very high degree of connection between outside and inside in architecture.'

TADAO ANDO

Defining idea…

149

How did
it go?

Q Given the cost and time involved in creating decking, is it not better to simply go the extra mile and create a stone terrace?

A   *It really depends on the type of property you have – and its value. With very high value, traditional style properties, it might make sense to create a more permanent feature. However, while decking doesn't necessarily score points for durability, it wins on flexibility. There are some buyers who will be so wowed by the sight of well planned decking that they won't care that it might not last for ever.*

Q Does a deck suit a classic English garden?

A   *No, not really – they are much better suited to a simple contemporary garden or one that has distinctly oriental influences. They look great with large scale, exotic looking plants. If, however, you do decide to combine a deck with a classic garden, create one that incorporates suitably decorative details such as trellising.*

Q Can decking be used to make paths?

A   *Yes, that is one of the great advantages of decking – you can create a seamless succession of walkways and sitting areas.*

The dangers of the much-loved house

It might make you the envy of your neighbours but creating a house that is the most expensive in the road can be dangerous strategy.

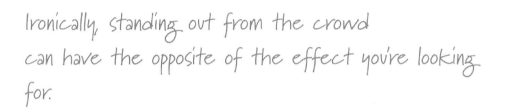

Ironically, standing out from the crowd can have the opposite of the effect you're looking for.

The overindulged house isn't hard to spot: the first sign is the front garden with not a single stone out of place. Next, you only need to look up to see the towering roof extension. Look further and you'll see most evidence: the giant back and side extension and the perfect decking – complete with expensive garden furniture, lead effect planters and a beautifully manicured lawn. 'But, but,' I hear you say 'surely all these things are the ambition of the buy-to-let speculator?' And of course, you'd be spot on; they are exactly that. But there is one important piece of missing information in all this – the house in question is in a street of undeveloped properties. And that's the problem; a house can be too perfect for the street in which it stands.

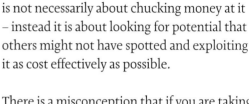

Here's an idea for you... **Keep a log of every house that comes on to the market in your area with a list of the features and the selling price (this latter piece of information will be available from the Land Registry a few months after the sale). Within six months or so, you'll have a very good idea of the different gradations in price and you'll be in a better position to decide what you should and shouldn't do to a property.**

The art of maximising the value of a property is not necessarily about chucking money at it – instead it is about looking for potential that others might not have spotted and exploiting it as cost effectively as possible.

There is a misconception that if you are taking a long term view, the rest of the houses will eventually catch up, so that it pays to get in there early, like one of America's early settlers. But that sort of speculation requires a vaulting leap of faith. Professional speculators tackle this problem by buying properties in an area and renting them out undeveloped until there are signs that the surrounding area is on the up. In the same way, any improvements that you make should only be in step with those of other houses in the street. It is fine to be the smartest house in the street if there are houses around that are almost as smart as yours.

Also remember that if you buy a house, develop it and then sit on it for five years, the chances are that by the time that you come to sell, any changes that you have made will have started to look pretty tired.

THE SECRETS OF UNDERSTANDING THE LOCAL MARKET

When buying a house only go through with it when you have looked at every property that has come on to the market in the last few months, so that you have a good idea what the potential might be. With the advent of the internet, it is also possible to glean enormous amounts of invaluable information about the local market without even visiting a property. Also, don't take one look at the number of skips in the road and think that this is definitely an area on the up – they might be developers who are turning properties into houses of multiple occupation.

After buying the property, when you're considering making major changes to a house always take into account what your neighbours are doing. Whenever a house comes on the market in the neighbourhood, you should always look around it to see the level of development. If you aren't completely confident that a market is ready to sustain a house with a huge lateral conversion, for example, then you should think twice before going ahead. However, you could try to predict future trends by examining the amount of development in a smarter area around the corner. If it looks like your area is going the same way then you might feel confident in taking a punt.

And a question you might want to consider is: how realistic is demand locally for the type of property in your mind's eye? Features such as wet rooms, decking and open plan living rooms might appeal to buyers in a sophisticated urban area, but might not necessarily attract buyers in a small provincial town.

'Never go to excess, but let moderation be your guide.'
MARCUS TULLIUS CICERO

Defining idea...

How did it go? **Q** **I'm confused. Surely if you are maximising the value of a prop-erty, it is important that you make it as desirable as you possibly can?**

A *Yes you should, but only up to a point. If the price of your house is 50% higher than any other house in the road you might find yourself with a problem, even if it does offer more bedrooms, a huge kitchen conserva-tory and ample off-street parking. The result will be that the undeveloped properties will suddenly look very cheap and many people will be tempted to do their own development. The secret is to be in a similar band to half a dozen other properties that have sold in the last couple of years.*

Q **But surely if I'm intending to stay for a while, the other houses will keep up?**

A *Possibly, but it's not a given. In areas where there's a lot of undeveloped housing, it is better to make gradual incremental improvements rather than giant leaps.*

35

Making a splash

Have you always wanted a swimming pool, but been afraid to take the plunge?

There are, of course, a few things that you need to consider before you splash the cash.

In everyone's mind there are some essential ingredients in the ideal property: a large garden, more bedrooms than you could shake a stick at, breathtaking views, nice neighbourhood – oh, and a shimmering, aquamarine swimming pool. But when it comes to creating an upmarket property, few developers question the value of a pool. Buyers, however, often take a rather different view.

Reservations might include the following:

1   *Maintenance.* For busy people without staff to do it for them, swimming pools are a time-consuming extra that need cleaning, maintenance and monitoring. In addition to all the other demands of running a large house and garden, looking after a swimming pool is just another responsibility.
2   *Running costs.* Swimming pools cost money to heat and keep clean. These are expenses that one might be happy to swallow if it is in constant use but it is harder to justify when it is only used on an occasional basis.

3   *Safety.* However safety conscious you are, swimming pools are always a hazard
     to small children.
4   *Space.* Unless a garden is more than an acre in size, a swimming pool will eat up
     a significant proportion of a garden.
5   *An unwanted added extra.* There is no doubt that there is a premium to be paid for
     a house with a swimming pool – and any potential buyer will be aware of this. If
     buyers are very keen to buy a house they will be happy to swallow the cost, but if
     there are a number of similar houses in the market, they might be more reluctant.

There will, of course, be cases where a pool will do an enormous amount to
enhance a property – particularly in an area of high value neighbouring houses
where they are a common feature. But remember that if a high value property has a
huge amount going for it in many other respects, a swimming pool won't necessarily make or break a deal – there are plenty of projects of a similar value that would
be more of an attraction, particularly those that require a huge amount of time and
effort to complete. If you're thinking of building a swimming pool as an investment
compare it with features such as an outbuilding that has been converted into independent accommodation for guests or a beau-
tifully designed home office. Also remember
that in the absence of a swimming pool, many
wealthy folk would be quite happy to build
one themselves, to their own specifications.

In mid-market properties a swimming pool
is unlikely to put much distance between
your house and others that might be on the
market – and in some cases it might be seen as
a negative feature.

Here's an idea for you... Once you've had an estimate for building a pool (remember to include the cost of any landscaping that may be involved as well as a pool house, if you need one) ask an estate agent who knows the type of house you live in for advice on whether it will add significantly to the value of your home.

INDOOR SWIMMING POOLS

While an indoor pool would seem to make a lot of sense in many respects they can be difficult to incorporate into period houses. In high value contemporary houses, they are can be a huge asset, but beware: they can create an appearance that some buyers might find a little … erm … vulgar.

HOT TUBS

Much of the point of a swimming pool is that it creates a pleasurable outdoor leisure activity (people rarely build them for exercise – swimming lanes in local swimming pools serve that purpose much more efficiently). Much of the reason for the growing popularity of hot tubs is that they offer some of the fun of a swimming pool, without the expense and headache. In the gardens of some period houses they may seem a little incongruous but in relaxed modern homes they are a great added extra.

SO SHOULD YOU TAKE THE PLUNGE?

There are two reasons why you might want to create a swimming pool: the first is because you want one for your own purposes; the other is to enhance a property in an area where they are the norm and a pool might be conspicuous by its absence. In any other scenario, it is hard to see that there will be a good return on your investment – it will possibly be a loss.

'Water is the driving force of all nature.'
LEONARDO DA VINCI

Defining idea…

How did it go?

Q   **But I just want a pool that will be fun for my children rather than as property investment. Is there any harm in that?**

A   *No, nothing at all. just don't try to con yourself that it will effectively pay for itself when you come to sell the property.*

Q   **Are there any planning implications involved in building a swimming pool?**

A   *There may be, particularly if the house is in a conservation area. Always check with the planning authorities first. Remember that there are some areas where local residents will raise objections if you so much as sneeze.*

Q   **I can't really see how a hot tub can be a substitute for a swimming pool.**

A   *It isn't really a substitute. It just has a few things in common, like the fact that swimming and sitting in a hot tub are both pleasurable ways of enjoying the great outdoors.*

36

Room to breathe

Forget immaculate herbaceous borders and a perfect lawn – the best asset a garden can offer is an 'outdoor room'.

For anyone refurbishing, a well planned outdoor room offers an opportunity to make a garden work harder.

In most modern homes the line between the inside and outside of a house has become somewhat blurred. Much of this is to do with architecture; time was when a garden could be reached via a back door and the only view out would have been limited to a single window. But now two significant changes have taken place. One is that we have opened up the back of our homes with either French windows or floor-to-ceiling sliding glass doors that allow us to enjoy our gardens whatever the weather – in addition it gives us much easier access to the outside. The second change is connected to the first; because we love the uninterrupted views from inside our homes, we also like an uninterrupted journey from one to the other, with the result that there is a growing fashion for bringing the level of the garden up to the level of the internal floor, creating a seamless join between one and the other.

Here's an idea for you... **When planning an outdoor room, treat the space in the same way that you would treat a room inside the house. Make a scale drawing of the proposed space and cut out representations of the different elements, such as such as tables, barbecues, etc.**

Both these changes have, in turn, had a dramatic impact on the way we treat our gardens – namely as an extension to our inside living space. In many cases the space immediately outside the back elevation of a house is less of a garden and more of an 'outdoor room.' These new rooms might not have four walls and a ceiling but they are designed in exactly the same way as an internal room. The fashion has had a variety of knock-on effects, namely a proliferation of 'domestic style' garden furniture, lighting and accessories.

And what's more the concept of another 'room' in the garden is a great option for smaller properties where additional entertaining space is a boon in the summer. But whatever the size of the property, the outer space helps to make the inner space seem much larger, too.

A word of warning though for those with a traditional style house: it is best to avoid a relentlessly contemporary look. Traditional terracing and balustrade will look much more in keeping with the rest of the property.

ESSENTIAL INGREDIENTS FOR AN OUTDOOR ROOM

- *Furniture.* Forget the austere, lichen-covered garden benches of yesteryear; outdoor rooms are furnished with sleek, comfortable 'sofas' and chairs with fabric covered pads.

- *Flooring*. Decking is a particular favourite, largely because it is more versatile and much more comfortable under foot than stone.
- *Lighting*. Fully wired up hanging lights are not unheard of but sleek integrated lighting is increasingly popular.
- *Fabrics*. There has been a proliferation in fabrics that will withstand life outdoors that create a much more sophisticated look than the canvas stripes of old. Ideal for benches, dining chairs and loungers.
- *Awnings/pergolas*. Awnings – basically large pieces of hemmed canvas – provide shade and a certain amount of protection from light showers. Another good way to create shade is with a pergola – a wooden frame built around and over the space, which creates an intimate feel that is ideal for meal times and entertaining.
- *Cooking equipment/heating*. A sleek barbecue is a must – some people have even fitted permanent outdoor kitchens, complete with work surfaces, fridges and sinks. In chilly weather, an outdoor heater or brazier helps to fend off the cold.

COOL CONCRETE

Increasingly, outdoor rooms are being created with the help of rendered breeze blocks and concrete. It is a quick, efficient way to create outdoor seating (with fabric covered pads for comfort). However, ensure that what you create won't look too out of date in a few years time – it always pays to err on the side of a classic look rather than the relentlessly contemporary.

'How fair is a garden amid the trials and passions of existence.'

BENJAMIN DISRAELI

Defining idea...

How did it go?

Q **What you're really talking about is a terrace, isn't it?**

A *I'm really talking about the modern version of a terrace. In the past, the most that you'd get on a terrace is a table and a few chairs. These days, they are treated much more as outdoor living spaces.*

Q **But how does a glorified patio really add to the value of a property?**

A *Because in this space-starved era in which we live, every square metre counts. And the way that people treat their gardens has changed dramatically in the last decade or so; these days they are seen as places to enjoy rather than toil over. And also an outdoor room is much more than a glorified patio; in good weather it is a living or dining room.*

Q **In a small garden, which is more important – an outdoor room or a beautiful lawn?**

A *An outdoor room, particularly if the property itself is pretty small, too.*

Q **I like the idea of a fabric awning but all the ones I've seen seem fantastically expensive.**

A *They needn't be. Companies that make covers for boats will run you up a simple awning to your own specification. You may need to add some posts to which it can be attached.*

37

High security

A good security system will add to the perceived value of your home.

And you don't have to live in a castle to keep the burglars at bay.

There's no doubt that in the property development game there are features that a potential buyer will be attracted to that they won't necessarily have considered installing in their own homes. Often, the reason for this is not because they don't want to, but because they never had the time, expertise – and possibly the budget – to have done so.

Good security is the perfect example of this. When one is developing a house it is very often a long way down the list of priorities; when you can't afford to fix the roof, the last thing that you consider doing is forking out for a security system. And it is easy to find reasons *not* to spend money on security, notably the philosophy that 'we haven't got anything to steal.' Yet, like many of the most valuable home improvements, installing a security system needn't be expensive – and it is much easier to install when a house is being refurbished.

Here's an idea for you... **Take a fresh look at your home from the perspective of a potential burglar, rather than a potential buyer. Which are the most likely points of entry to the property, are there any windows that are easily accessed and need better security? Write a list of all security related issues that need to be tackled.**

Yet good security isn't just about hi-tech systems, it is also about some surprisingly simple devices such as window locks, which despite being relatively inexpensive, all help to create a reassuring impression when buyers come to view a property.

While planning the security of a property, it is worth researching any stipulations that an insurance company might have. In some cases they may demand that you have an alarm system and specify precisely what features it has.

Here are some key security-related points to consider when you are developing a property.

- *Alarm systems.* These range from the basic to the very sophisticated. The more expensive domestic systems will be monitored by an alarm company who will contact you – and in some cases your local police station – in the event of a burglary. Remember that companies offering a monitoring system will charge a monthly fee for their services.
- *CCTV.* CCTV is an acronym for closed-circuit television and describes a system that allows you to monitor your property and keep recordings of any activity. Once the preserve of commercial premises, these are now a common feature of domestic security systems. You may be surprised at how affordable a CCTV system can be – it can also act as a very effective deterrent.

- *Entrance gates.* In the case of a house with a perimeter fence or wall and in its own plot, you can't beat a pair of large electric gates with an intercom, and possibly a CCTV camera.
- *Perimeter fence/wall.* When building perimeter walls or fences it is important that you take them as high as possible – the maximum height will be stipulated by local planning regulations. Brick walls are ruinously expensive but might be a good investment in very high value properties (particularly if neighbouring properties have them). A less expensive option is brick walls on the side of the property that faces the road and wooden fencing elsewhere.
- *Gravel.* Gravel is not only a very cost effective option for driveways it is also a very low-tech form of security: because of the noise it creates it announces the arrival of visitors – and burglars.

SOME OTHER POINTS TO CONSIDER

There are, of course, plenty of other benefits to having electric gates and good perimeter walls or fencing – they provide a safe, secure, private environment for children and pets. However, remember that care must be taken with children and electric gates – never allow a child near a gate that shuts automatically.

Also, bear in mind that a property fitted with hi-tech alarms and CCTV cameras might create the impression that security is a problem. There are some properties where this level of security would look perfectly natural – but others where it will stick out like a sore thumb.

'There's no point shutting the door after the horse has bolted.'

Defining idea...

PROVERB

How did
it go?

Q **I'm confused! On the one hand you are saying that good security is a big advantage in a property, on the other you seem to be saying that it might send out the wrong message about the area. So which is it?**

A *It's a question of degree, really – and also the type of property that you have. What you need to be wary of is creating a property that looks – and feels – like the US embassy in Baghdad. If the property is in a dodgy neighbourhood, high visibility security will simply emphasise the point. There are some security features, such as half a dozen CCTV cameras and security wiring that will look grim. However, electric gates and one or two CCTV cameras will simply look reassuring.*

Q **I can't really afford an alarm system at the moment. Are there any short term measures, I could take?**

A *Yes. Ensure that you have the best possible locks that you can afford. You might also consider having a fake alarm box. You can now also buy fake CCTV cameras.*

Q **Will the fact that a house doesn't have a sophisticated security system be a deal breaker?**

A *Not necessarily, but it is one of those elements that will combine with other features to create a house that is greater than the sum of its parts. Also, remember that in the grand scheme of things, a good security system is relatively inexpensive.*

38

Hidden dangers

The best surveyors tend to be the most pessimistic.

However, they will also help you prioritise
work that needs doing most urgently.
Ignore their advice at your peril.

When developing a property, it's tempting to devote your time and effort – and put your money – into high profile projects. But the truth is that you should seek the help of a good surveyor (ideally a pessimistic one), who will highlight essential issues such as damp, plumbing and wiring.

The surveyor is the one professional who is just as important to the successful refurbishment of a property as a good builder or architect. To many people – particularly those on a tight budget – a survey is just another of those irritating boxes that needs to be ticked when you are buying a property. In fact, good surveyors are the key ingredient in any successful development. They will not only identify potential problems but will also be on hand to offer impartial advice as you make important decisions. In this respect, a surveyor can offer advice that is far more astute and more dispassionate than either a builder or a architect who are likely to have some hidden agenda (i.e. those that relate to any issues that might make them more money, cause inconvenience, take more time or look any better in their portfolio).

Here's an idea for you... **A good starting point in a search for a surveyor is a professional body. However, don't limit yourself to this source; personal recommendation can be just as good. Ask as many of the estate agents or solicitors you are dealing with for recommendations. Some will just suggest friends, but if there are names that come up consistently, the chances are that there'll be a good reason.**

As you develop a property it is essential that you keep on referring back to the findings and recommendations of a surveyor's report. Also, don't be afraid to ask your surveyor back to give advice on any projects that you might be planning or any other issues that you might have encountered. The cost of a good survey – and any subsequent advice that they might give – is a trifle when compared to the value that they can add to a property.

When appointing a surveyor, it is important that you find one who has a good knowledge of the area where the property stands. Not only will a surveyor with local knowledge be in a good position to highlight any issues relating to environmental or development issues – they will also be able to offer advice on any planning applications that you are hoping to make, either at the time of the sale or in the future. The chances are that the surveyor will also have already surveyed the property – or a neighbouring property that is very similar.

THE CONTENTS OF A SURVEY

It goes without saying that whatever property you are buying, it is essential that you have a full structural survey rather than just a valuation. As well as giving an opinion on the price of a property, a full structural survey will look at the condition of both the building and the plot in which it stands. The areas that it will cover include

- Access/rights of way
- History of the property
- Quality of construction (including any materials used)
- Structural issues (i.e. subsidence)
- Drainage
- Electrics
- Roof
- Damp
- Dry rot
- Wet rot
- Woodworm

The result will be a document that is illustrated with photographs and, for an average house, should be about 40–50 pages long.

THE WAY FORWARD

Once you've bought the property, you then need to decide which issues you intend to tackle – and any that you feel can either be postponed or ignored completely. Remember that surveyors are paid to be pessimistic, so there may be issues that won't need to be remedied while you are in the property. But if you discuss what your plans are, a surveyor should give you a list of what the main priorities are. Another hallmark of a good surveyor is one who is capable of lateral thought and who will help you find practical solutions that you might not have thought of yourself.

'A pessimist is one who makes difficulties of his opportunities and an optimist is one who makes opportunities of his difficulties.'

HARRY S TRUMAN

Defining idea...

169

However tempting it might be to believe that it is glistening new bathrooms, and light-filled extensions that will wow a potential buyer, it is their surveyor's report that will be the grim voice of reason – a voice that could easily scupper a sale or be used as a reason to renegotiate the price.

How did it go?

Q **Surely a potential buyer will be far more blown away by the sight of a beautiful gleaming, state-of-the-art kitchen than a glowing surveyor's report?**

A *You may find a buyer who doesn't care about the condition of the fabric of the building but it is a huge risk to take – and even then you will be massively narrowing down your target market. The other problem with ignoring issues such as damp and structural problems is that if they become so bad that a remedy is unavoidable, you may end up having to rip out any work that you have already done. It really doesn't make any sense to cut corners when issues such as this are concerned. If you can't afford the work – don't buy the property.*

Q **What is a good example of lateral thought when faced with a bad survey?**

A *Well, if an extension requires so much damp proofing (believe me the costs can escalate) you may decide that the money is better spent knocking it down and starting again. A good surveyor should help you to weigh up these options and to identify any ideas that are practical.*

39

Child's play

Creating a practical and attractive playroom might not be as effortless as you imagine.

But the secret of success is to keep it safe and simple and let your kids make it their own.

There's no doubt that a dedicated children's playroom is a luxury that will be a huge draw to potential buyers. But while it might be tempting to throw all your money and creative energies into an elaborate children's fantasy world, resist the urge at all costs. The best playrooms are those that are a triumph not of style over function but function over style.

The golden rules of creating a great child's playroom are threefold:

1   Wherever possible the playroom should adjoin the kitchen.
2   Children have a short attention span and will quickly tire of elaborate elements such as a pirate's ship and fancy murals. It is better to create a well-designed, functional space where they can create their own fun. Also, remember that children grow up quickly, so anything too ornate may date quickly.
3   It is essential that you create plenty of low-level desk space for drawing, home-work and using computers.

LAYOUT AND DECORATIVE FEATURES

When you're planning the playroom, consider the following.

■ *Walls*. While there isn't any reason why you shouldn't go wilder and wackier than you might do in any other room, it pays to keep the look restrained. One very good reason for this is that when potential purchasers visit the property, it will be easier for them to envisage the room being used for some other purpose – such as dining room, living room or media room. The most important factor in the decoration of a playroom is that the walls are robust enough to stand up to the battering that they will inevitably be subjected to. Remember that when wallpaper is scratched or drawn on it is difficult to repair (even if your own children are forbidden to do this, someone else's inevitably will). Try to fix a large number of magnetic notice boards – infinitely preferable to blue tack

Here's an idea for you... **If you're looking for inspiration whilst creating the ideal environment for a child, take a look at how the professionals do it. When visiting nurseries and schools for your children always look for design ideas – they tend to be the result of years of experience.**

and drawing pins. If you want to create a distinctive look you could consider painting two or three walls in white and the remainder in some vibrant accent colour that could be played on elsewhere.

■ *Flooring*. While carpet is ideal for babies and toddlers, it causes problems when children start becoming creative. If using carpet, lay rugs on top – or lay carpet tiles. The most practical flooring is wood, lino or vinyl, but again use rugs to soften them.

Because children spend so much time on the floor, the ideal combination would be a functional surface with underfloor heating.

■ *Furniture*. Other than basic tables and chairs for toddlers, most children's furniture becomes obsolete very quickly. The best bet is a folding table or two – these can be put away when you need to maximise space – and a comfortable sofa or two. Another essential ingredient is plenty of bean bags and/or floor cushions.

■ *Storage*. For the sake of aesthetics – and your sanity – it is essential that you invest heavily in plenty of cupboard space, preferably fitted. As well as storing toys and craft materials, you could also create a section that is devoted to any other purpose that the room is used for (see below).

■ *Windows*. Simple curtains are the best bet – beware of blinds with hanging cords, they are a danger to small children.

THE MULTIFUNCTIONAL PLAYROOM

Inevitably, there will be times when you want a playroom to serve a dual purpose such as a

'The reluctance to put away childish things may be a requirement of genius.'
REBECCA PEPPER SINKLER

Defining idea...

home office, spare bedroom or dining room. For those who only need a space to work after their children's bed time – or a dining room half a dozen times a year, a playroom offers the perfect opportunity to create a flexible space. It is for this reason that plenty of storage is essential.

THE 'VIRTUAL' PLAYROOM

In some cases there will be times when you are unwilling – or possibly unable – to devote an entire room to a playroom. In this case it is essential that you create a large amount of storage near the main reception rooms that can be disgorged, as and when toys are required.

Q **Isn't the style of playroom that you're advocating a little dull and functional?**

How did it go?

A *It will be dull when you first put it together but it is far better to create a simple backdrop, which can then evolve with the changing tastes and interests of your children. Once they have put their artwork and posters on the walls it will look anything but dull. Sadly, the attractions of anything too elaborate will soon wear thin. And, yes, it will be functional but plenty of floor cushions and bean bags in jolly colours will soon jazz it up. However, there's another reason to keep the look quite simple and that is because it will allow potential purchasers see the possibilities of it having various different functions.*

Q **So, not even a pretty Wendy house with gingham curtains, then?**

A *To be honest you can put anything you like in the playroom as long as it isn't a permanent fixture – flexibility is all.*

40

Classic or contemporary?

Interior design is polarised between two very different styles.

So the question is: which one has the most universal appeal?

A quarter of a century ago the answer to this conundrum would have been very different – and probably a lot more straightforward, too. Back then, there was an unwritten convention that you decorated a house according to its period and architectural style. So, if you had a grand Georgian house, the style you would choose would be a loose modern interpretation of grand Georgian – swagged curtain plus real or reproduction 18th century furniture. If it was Victorian, you might choose gothic furniture. And if it was modern, you'd opt for a clean-lined minimal look.

But these days it's not quite as simple as that. Now, almost anything goes and we tend to be much less hung up on choosing a style that is necessarily sympathetic to the style of the building. And we are much more comfortable about mixing styles too. But in a sense, more freedom has created more of a headache for anyone developing a property.

Here's an idea for you... **The only way to identify the style that you want is to create a 'mood board': collect together images that show rooms in the style that you want to achieve (take colour photocopies from books if you don't want to tear them up). You could also add samples of fabric, flooring and wallpaper that you might also use. The result will give you a pretty good idea of the scheme that you're aiming for.**

CHOOSING A STYLE

The most important rule when choosing a style for a property is to think less about the house and more about the market that you are targeting. If a property is most likely to sell to a young first time buyer, then it makes sense to go for quite an urban, contemporary look. If, however, the property is a large, traditional house in the country, then it makes sense to opt for a style that will appeal to those with more conventional tastes. Yet even that approach has its perils. It would be unwise to create a look that is so relentlessly modern – or traditional – that you alienate those niche customers who break the mould. There may be funky young things looking for large country houses and mature, country types hoping to downshift to a small flat in town.

The secret is to create an environment (i.e. walls and floors) that is as simple and pared down as possible and to furnish it in a way that will appeal to your core market. The result will be a sufficiently versatile scheme that people will be able to envisage living in whatever their taste.

CREATING A VERSATILE BACKDROP

It is worth remembering that when many period houses were originally built, they were decorated in quite a simple, pared down way that might seem modern today. It is only the grander Georgians and Victorians who liked to stuff a house to the gunnels.

The environment you create should be where classic and contemporary meet in the middle. Avoid white – or anything approaching it – at all costs. Conversely, rich period colours are also a no-no. Stones, creams and aquas are all ideal. Too much exposed wood, particularly pine, should also be avoided. The only exception is hardwood floors – and light coloured stone or linoleum is ideal for kitchens. Kitchens and fitted joinery should be simple, too – the shaker look is ideal for this purpose and can easily be painted by new owners who want a more traditional feel.

FURNISHING TO TARGET YOUR CORE MARKET

Against this backdrop you can now inject schemes that will appeal to whoever it is that you regard as your target buyer. But even then it is a good idea to take a 'centrist' approach, rather than going to either of the extremes. For example, if decorating a dining room in a classic style with 18th century furniture, you should tone it down with fabrics and paints in a muted palette of colours. Equally, you run the risk of alienating a significant part of your market if you create a living room that looks like the interior of the *Starship Enterprise.* Balance is all.

'Simplicity is the ultimate sophistication.'
LEONARDO DA VINCI

Defining idea…

How did it go? **Q** **I've decided to go for a style that will suit the younger market. However, does that mean that I'll have to wave goodbye to my collection of antique furniture, much of it inherited from family?**

    A *No, not necessarily; the point that I was making was that as long as the property is stylistically a 'half-way house', potential purchasers will be able to envisage putting their own stamp on it. That said, if you have a lot of antiques and the overall feel is quite quirky or eccentric, they might not be able to see beyond it. You might decide that it is better to 'edit' your furniture. You don't need to get rid of it. You could simply rent a storage unit while you create a look with more universal appeal.*

    Q **Goodness, it all sounds like a huge upheaval. Is it really necessary?**

    A *It could be argued that many of the suggestions here aren't completely necessary. The problem is that when the time comes to sell, your property might be up against other houses that have a look that will appeal to a broader spectrum of people. It is surprising how much difference such apparently superficial considerations can make.*

Film stars

'Media rooms' are no longer the preserve of movie moguls; advances in technology mean that it is possible to create your own silver screen experience close to home.

And you probably won't need the space to seat the cast and crew of the film you're watching either.

A 'media room' is a very grand name for what we use to call the 'telly room' or even the 'snug'. What has transformed these humble, cosy rooms is technology; rather that the basic television and video recorder of old, we now have access to flat screen TVs, DVDs, PlayStations, satellite channels and sophisticated 'wraparound' sound systems that recreate a similar quality to a professional cinema.

The joy of a media room is that it offers a great way to enhance space that you already have. For example, if you have a classic double-ended living room, it is relatively simple to give it new purpose by turning it into a dedicated media room. The other attraction of a media room is that it is a great way to use small, irregular spaces that might not have much light (i.e. in basements).

Before you embark on finding space for a media room, draw a plan of the configuration that you'd ideally like to create. The minimum elements that need to be included in the scheme are: a screen, plus supporting equipment and sofa. So you may be surprised at the small spaces that you could consider for a media room. This process might also give you an idea of some other function that a media room might perform, such as a home office.

ESSENTIAL INGREDIENTS

■ *Technology.* As well as the obvious, it is worth considering installing hi-fi equipment in a media room. In a complete refurbishment of a house, it is relatively simple to install wiring that will take sound to other parts of the house. The most important factor when planning where equipment should go, is that it should ideally be out of sight, particularly any wiring that is required. The starting point of any design should always be the ideal configuration of the speakers – manufacturers offer advice on this.

- *Furniture*. Because media rooms are often quite small, it makes sense to use modular furniture – i.e. sofas that are made of units that allow you to custom-ise them to suit the space (there is also a limit to the amount of furniture that you need). The classic item of modular furniture is a basic 'L' shaped sofa that allows you to sit, sprawl or lie in a variety of different positions, with the result that it is ideal for watching, television or reading. However, a more space effi-cient option would be units of upholstered seating that run around the walls of a room.
- *Decoration*. Even in a traditionally decorated house, it makes sense to create a media room that has quite a sleek contemporary feel. Dark colours work well on the walls, as do simple blinds. A fitted unit or low cabinet that can accom-modate audio visual unit is idea. Low lighting is important, but remember to create some overhead lighting (i.e. low voltage spot lights) for cleaning.

THE MULTIPURPOSE MEDIA ROOM

There are a variety of other functions that a media rooms can serve. It is the ideal place, for example, to fit book shelves. If you create a lot of storage it is also the ideal place to base a 'virtual home office' where you keep a laptop, hard drive, printer and any filing that you might need. Also, for those who love entertaining, it is a great place to create a dedicated drinks cupboard with glasses, bot-tles and possibly a small fridge (punters love this sort of detail). With good storage, it is also

'If a man insisted always on being serious, and never allowed himself a bit of fun and relaxation, he would go mad or become unstable without knowing it.'

HERODOTUS

Defining idea...

183

possible to create a room that is a play room by day and a media room at night – but remember that you'll have to train children to put everything away at bedtime.

THE HOME CINEMA

In a high value property, you may be tempted to create a home cinema with a couple of rows of seats. Like the swimming pool, it is one of those high cost luxuries that may appeal to some potential buyers but will be viewed with suspicion by others. And like the swimming pool, the home cinema is a feature that should be regarded as a personal indulgence rather than an investment that will add value to a property.

Q   What you are really talking about is a TV room isn't it?

A   A TV room is somewhere that you happen to keep the TV – a media room is a place that is specifically designed to maximise the enjoyment you get out of watching television or listening to music. The difference has really been driven by technology that allows you create a cinema style experience for a fraction of what it might have cost ten years ago.

Q   Isn't the difference more about semantics than technology?

A   It's actually about style. Media rooms tend to offer home owners an opportunity to create a sleek, contemporary feel, even if the rest of the house is quite classic.

Q   I want to fix a plasma screen to the wall but it rather compromises the configuration of furniture in the room – basically, it means that I have to have the sofa directly in front of it.

A   It's often better to have plasma screens that are on their own self supporting unit, so that that they can be angled to suit the layout of the room.

How did it go?

42

Up for rent

In some areas, you might decide that the best market for your property is as a rental investment.

Many of the principles of preparing your property for rent are the same as for preparing to sell.

The secret of any successful development is to decide which target market your property suits best, and then to tailor it accordingly – whether it's for a first time buyer or an affluent family. In some cases you may decide that the best prospect for a property is as a rental. There are a variety of reasons that owners decide to do this – as an investment, because of a change in circumstances (you may be moving abroad for a couple of years) – or because so many other properties have gone the same way that you are unlikely to be able to sell it for any other purpose. Alternatively, you may decide to develop a property so that it is attractive to a buy-to-let investor.

The buy-to-let market has grown exponentially in recent years, with the number of properties swollen by landlords who buy flats 'off plan' (i.e. before they are built) and then let them out. The market has been driven by two factors, one of which is relatively low interest rates that allow landlords a healthy margin between their outgoings and their income – and also by private individuals who are looking for

Here's an idea for you... **Talk to letting agents about which properties are in the highest demand. The most important factor is how quickly properties rent; if you have too many void periods you may find yourself making a loss.**

alternative forms of investment to the stock market or pension schemes. Sadly, the world of the buy-to-let is not all a bed of roses. The two biggest dangers include high interest rates and oversupply in the particular market that you are targeting (i.e. too many two bedroom flats in a town where there are a high number of new apartment blocks).

Nevertheless, risks aside, there will be occasions and properties that lend themselves to a buy to let investment.

THE SECRETS OF A SUCCESSFUL RENTAL

1   While it doesn't make sense to throw money at a buy-to-let, it is also a false economy to cut corners. Not only will a clean, functional fit out make the property more desirable to potential tenants, it will also cost less to maintain.
2   It is better to buy new inexpensive furniture, rather than secondhand items from house clearance – and contemporary is always a better bet than traditional, even in period houses.
3   If re-decorating, always use white paint as it is easier to touch up between rentals.
4   When buying upholstered furniture, try to buy a model which comes with spare covers so that you can replace them further down the line.
5   Always check with the local council to see whether the property needs any licences/regulations associated with the property – i.e. if you are letting to a group of individuals it might qualify as a House Of Multiple Occupation (HMO) which will be governed by a rigorous list of regulations.

6   Ensure that the garden is low maintenance. Shrubs and herbaceous borders will require work. In small gardens, you may be better off with gravel.

7   It rarely makes sense to invest very heavily in kitchen units – if there is a kitchen already in place, simply replace any tired work tops and replace (or paint) any doors.

WHO DO I RENT TO?

One question you might need to ask is: is it better to create an HMO or a property that will be rented by a family? While there is likely to be a higher return on an HMO that is in an area of low value houses, your initial outlay is likely to be higher because of the strict requirements that have to be met. However, once you've created an HMO it will also be expensive to revert it to a property that is suitable for families. There may also be more wear and tear.

On the other hand, the rental return might not be as good on a family house but the chances are that the appreciation might be better. The danger with HMOs is that when there are a large number in close proximity, property values may become depressed.

THE MAGIC RENTAL FORMULA

There is a formula used by buy-to-let landlords when they are deciding whether or not to invest in an area. They believe that the key to success is to identify a town or city that has a large population under the age of 30 and a small supply of buy-to-let properties. If a town has a large student population, that tends to be pretty good bet, too.

'Property has its duties as well as its rights.'

THOMAS DRUMMOND

Defining idea…

How did it go?

Q Surely buying a new build property will offer years of maintenance free rental?

A *There are three problems with new builds: the first is that there is often oversupply with the result that there is a lot of competition for tenants. The second is that they are expensive relative to older properties. The third is that they don't offer any opportunities to add value. You will achieve much higher yields on properties that you can develop yourself.*

Q What about renting high value properties?

A *The market for luxury properties can be a little more precarious because there are fewer potential tenants. You only need a couple of void months to take a significant slice out of your profits. That said, if you think that there's potential for long term growth – and you can cover the cost of maintenance and interest rates – any losses should be covered by rising values.*

43

A short commute

It might just look like a glorified shed but creating an office in the garden can be a huge asset.

And the psychological impact of the journey to work is significant even when the office is just beyond the vegetable patch.

When developing a property, it pays to examine ways that you can add to the amount of accommodation. The obvious – and costly – way to achieve this is with an extension, either at ground level or in attic spaces. But there are plenty of other ways to add room, including converting outhouses and even garages. One increasingly popular means of adding space is to build a prefabricated cabin in the garden. This kind of development is most commonly used as a home office. In many cases, construction can require little more than the basic unit being lowered into the garden on a crane and then fitted out. There are a growing number to choose from, most of which can be constructed in a couple of days – and, if necessary can be wired and plumbed to provide a small kitchen and bathroom if necessary.

Here's an idea for you... **The internet is awash with the websites of companies that offer garden offices. Don't just look at those that are available locally. The sites of foreign companies will give you a good idea of the possibilities and you might decide to create a bespoke design of your own rather than buying 'off the peg'.**

The growth in popularity of garden cabins has been driven by the way that we work; technological advances have meant that it is much easier to run a business or work part of the week at home. A self-contained space, away from the house can create an ideal working environment, particularly for those with families.

Within the context of property development, the value of a garden cabin is far greater than it might at first seem. As well as creating secondary accommodation, a cabin will unleash a significant amount of space from the main house. Not only will it free up a ground floor room or bedroom but it also provides storage for books, files and any other overflow items from that you can find a home for.

What is crucial when choosing a cabin is that it fits into its environment. Most cabins are aesthetically very pleasing, but do what you can to ensure that it looks like part of the garden – trellis and climbing plants will help it to blend into its surroundings. In some cases you may also want to give it its own deck, possibly joining it to the main house with a decking walkway.

Inevitably, not all potential purchasers will want to use your cabin as a home office – some may see it as a glorified garden store, workshop, summer house or just a convenient form of storage. In some cases it can be used as extra accommodation.

However, there is no doubt that whatever use it is put to, it will be regarded as an asset. The only factor that you should be aware of is that a cabin shouldn't compromise the rest of the garden. In small gardens, you should try to find a space where its impact is limited.

DECORATING A GARDEN CABIN OFFICE

Space efficiency and storage are the key factors in designing the interior of a garden cabin. The most efficient configuration is one long fitted work surface that runs along the length of the space. On the wall above, fit a large area of noticeboard with shelving behind it. On the other wall fit floor-to-ceiling shelves that will maximise the amount of filing and books that you can 'decant' from the main house.

As for the outside, if you're planning to paint, then you need look no further for inspiration than the chattel houses of the Caribbean. However, bright colours might not suit some properties. One colour that can look very smart and discreet is black.

SECURITY

Because a cabin is away from the main house, there will always be a high risk of burglary. It is important that you take the same precautions that you take with the main house; fit good quality locks on doors and windows and, most crucially, movement-sensitive security lights. Ideally, work on a laptop that you can take inside at night – or if you have a permanent arrangement, ensure

'Talents are best nurtured in solitude.'

GOETHE

Defining idea...

193

that you back up files on a regular basis so that you are never in danger of losing work.

Q   A lot of the garden cabins I've come across look like an inside out sauna. Is there anything I can do?

A   You'll be able to create a cabin with a slightly more urbane look if you paint it – but remember that this will involve much more maintenance.

Q   Will I need planning permission to create a cabin in the garden?

A   Some will and some won't, so it's wise to check with your local planning office. Planning controls have less to do with the size of the structure that you are planning to build and more to do with the purpose that you'll be using it for.

Q   I like the idea of using a cabin as overflow accommodation. Is there a problem with insulation?

A   Not in a high quality build. Remember that in some parts of the world people live in wooden buildings all year round in freezing temperatures. However, if you use a cabin as living accommodation it might be subject to different planning regulations.

44

Kitchen layout made easy

There's no mystery to designing a great kitchen – just a few basic principles and lots of common sense.

In many people's minds, the kitchen is the very heart of the house, so it's important to get it right!

Many homeowners labour under the misconception that kitchen design is a complex art. In fact, it simply relies on following a few basic rules and tailoring some tried and tested formulas to your own purposes. Of course, there will be properties and situations in which you'll want to call on the services of a designer but, if you're working with a straightforward layout – or have a limited budget, there is no reason why you shouldn't tackle the task yourself. Another great help is the large number of web-based programs created by kitchen suppliers that will help you to decide which configuration you need.

Obviously, the design of your kitchen will be governed by its size, but don't be constrained by the current dimensions of the kitchen area. You may be planning to increase the space by building an extension or annexing another room, so your kitchen design should go hand-in-glove with the potential for expansion. Why not

Here's an idea for you... **Search the internet for the most user-friendly kitchen planning programmes. You'll find them on the websites of most of the large kitchen suppliers. They are an invaluable free resource and you should make the most of them. You can, of course, just use old fashioned graph paper but a kitchen design programme will make you aware of the main issues involved.**

start with a sketch of your ideal kitchen, even if it doesn't relate to the existing space?

However, what we are mainly looking at here has less to do with the space itself and more to do with the way that cabinetry is arranged.

LAYOUT

The successful design of any kitchen, however big or small, relies on creating an uninterrupted triangle between the three 'activity zones' for food preparation, cooking and serving, each with their own dedicated work surfaces, storage, appliances and services. For maximum efficiency, the total length of the three sides of the triangle should be no more than 3600–6600mm and, wherever possible, any movement should be uninterrupted by through traffic.

This triangle should be the foundation upon which any kitchen is planned.

There are five basic layouts to consider:

1   *Corridor.* This layout is ideal for long, narrow spaces. If you are planning to position rows of worktops and appliances opposite one another, you will need

at least 1200mm between each row. If this isn't possible you should consider fitting worktops and appliances against just one wall.

2   *L-shaped.* This is a great solution for kitchens where worktops and appliances can all be installed in one corner.

3   *U-shaped.* This is perhaps the ideal layout as all appliances are then within easy reach. Ensure that there is at least 1200mm between both sides of the U shape.

4   *Island.* In a kitchen where there is plenty of room an island provides a central workspace around which to manoeuvre. It is a popular format, as it makes cooking more of a sociable activity. If you choose to install an appliance or sink in an island, remember to allow for the provision of plumbing, electricity and/ or gas.

5   *Peninsula.* When space is limited, this layout offers many of the advantages of an island but the central work space is connected to other units. It is ideal if there isn't sufficient space for an island unit.

WALL MOUNTED UNITS

If space allows, try to avoid fitting wall units as they can make a room feel enclosed. It is better to create a large adjoining larder where you can store food, and china (it makes sense to keep pans and cooking utensils near the oven or range).

WINDOWS

When planning a layout, remember that the kitchen sink is best positioned next to a window, as a view will offer a welcome distraction whilst washing up. Window treatments should never detract from the kitchen's role as a functional machine; blinds take up a minimum of space.

'To create architecture is to put in order. Put what in order? Function and objects.'
LE CORBUSIER

Defining idea…

How did
it go?

Q   Are you implying that there's no need to pay for a professionally designed kitchen?

A   *No. If your budget allows – and you are developing a high value property – it's a great investment. There is really no comparison between a top-of-the-range kitchen and one that uses standard units. You also get more than just the services of a designer – you get great craftsmanship and materials. However, if it's just a basic kitchen you are looking for, there's no reason that you can't design the layout yourself (with a lot of thought and effort).*

Q   Surely having fitted wall units makes the best use of space?

A   *Yes it does – but the overall appearance of the kitchen will be much more pleasing if you can manage it. When you estimate the total amount of space in wall-mounted cupboards you might find that it is easy to accommodate a comparable amount of space elsewhere.*

Q   I like the idea of unfitted units as I can take them with me. Are they a good idea?

A   *The prospect of kitchen units not being included in a sale will definitely put a black mark against your property. Also remember that fitted units tend to make a much better use of space than unfitted.*

45

Lighting

Good lighting is one of the most important elements in any successful refurbishment.

No doubt you'll find the following ideas wonderfully illuminating.

Too often lighting is an afterthought: 'Oh, now that we've painted the walls and laid some flooring, we need a few lamps.' No approach could spell greater disaster for a scheme. Because lighting is such an intangible element in a room, we tend to shy away from thinking about it too long and hard; yet if we take a logical approach nothing could be more straightforward. One important rule when planning a lighting scheme is to try to create a variety of different light sources that will give you the greatest flexibility.

There are, broadly speaking, five different types of lighting:

1   *Ambient lighting.* This is a cover-all term for overhead light that can be created with either hanging lights or lights that have been inset into the ceiling. Unless you want to make a statement with a chandelier (see below) the best type of ambient lighting is a low voltage spot light that is fitted in a recessed unit in the ceiling. Low voltage lighting creates a cleaner, more even light than a pendant light (a light that hangs on flex that is fitted with a shade) and doesn't intrude on the space to the same extent. Ambient light should always be fitted with a dimmer switch.

When planning a scheme, it is essential that you mark the position of existing and proposed lighting on a scale drawing. If you are considering table lamps, it is essential that there is a socket nearby. If you have a lamp on a table, you may want to consider fixing a socket in the floor, so that that you don't have wires trailing across the carpet.

It is tempting to think that you can do without a strong overhead light, particularly if there is a good source of natural light. In fact, overhead light is essential for cleaning, or in rooms such as halls and kitchens where you need a variety of different light sources for different activities.

The only downside to low voltage spots is that they are expensive to fit and expensive to maintain.

2   *Task lighting.* As the name suggests, task lighting is for a specific purpose such as reading, cooking and shaving. When planning a scheme it is important to identify which tasks you'll be carrying out where, so that you can plan accordingly. Well-planned task lighting is particularly important in a kitchen, where good low level lighting is essential.

3   *Mood lighting.* Lighting plays more than a purely functional role in a scheme. Plenty of low level lighting in the form of table and standard lamps lend a room a pleasing, mellow feel. Remember that table lamps need to be placed on a surface, which can restrict a layout; it is often easier to have mood lighting that is independent of furniture such as standard lamps and can offer more flexibility.

4   *Statement lighting.* This includes chandeliers and wall lights that serve a decorative purpose and should be treated with care when creating a scheme that

is intended to appeal to as many potential buyers as possible. In a hallway or formal living room, a hanging light should reflect the prevailing style of the house but beware of anything too quirky. Simple wall lights are a great way to enhance the look of both contemporary and classic schemes. They also have the advantage of not requiring either floor or table space.

5   *Architectural lighting.* In many pared down contemporary interiors, you can use light as a decorative feature in the scheme, lighting elements such as walls, staircases and niches.

THE DANGERS OF THE OVERLIT INTERIOR

In high value developments there is a temptation to 'gild the lily' with lighting. However, remember that too much fancy lighting can make a property look like an expensive hotel – and could also be inappropriate in many traditionally decorated period homes.

OUTDOOR LIGHTING

As well as playing an important functional role, particularly in welcoming visitors and for security, outdoor lighting can be a key element in garden design. Consider lighting trees, shrubs and water features – but remember that an overlit garden won't make you popular with neighbours.

Also remember that since most viewings – particularly in summer – take place in day-light, elaborate outdoor lighting will have only a limited impact on the value of a house.

'In the right light at the right time, everything is extraordinary.'

AARON ROSE

Defining idea...

LIGHTING AND VIEWINGS

If you have a lighting scheme that you are proud of, brief the estate agent to point it out to potential buyers. Also, leave some lighting on, even if viewings are in daylight. However, too much lighting may suggest that you have a problem with natural light.

Q **On the one hand you say that it is important to create lots of sources of light, but on the other you say that one should not have too much. Isn't this a contradiction in terms?**

A *When it comes to fancy lighting, you can have too much of a good thing. Because there have been such leaps and bounds in lighting technology recently many designers treat the techniques that are available like a new toy. As in all things, moderation is all.*

Q **I've had a quote for low voltage lighting and it seems exorbitant. Is it really worth the money?**

A *Yes it is – but only in areas that warrant it. If budgets are tight, only put it in those places where it will have most impact, such as halls, living rooms, bathrooms and kitchens.*

46

Lifestyle for sale

The most successful properties don't just offer great kitchens, bathrooms and living rooms – they offer buyers a whole new way of life.

So why not capitalise on what advertising agencies have known for years?

We all love a quick fix. Pick up almost any glossy magazine and they are full of easy solutions to life's problems. And the fact that we all buy them in droves, suggest that we love the concept. The best property developments are those that play on the same common human desire for a perfect lifestyle. For evidence of this fact, you only need to look at the advertising for new apartment blocks. They don't just show pictures of the bedrooms and bathrooms, they show pictures of people eating, drinking, entertaining. They aren't just selling property, they're selling a lifestyle.

The reason that professional developers use these techniques is because they are proven to work and it makes sense to take a leaf out of their book. Of course, when you come to sell a property you don't create a poster campaign. What you should do, however, is sell a lifestyle to which a potential buyer aspires.

Here's an idea for you... **In order to emphasise the lifestyle aspect of a property you should consider making a PowerPoint slideshow that can run on a loop as people look around a property. This is particularly useful in the winter months when you may be able to show images of light-filled interiors, a deck and possibly a leafy garden.**

A beautifully presented property is rather like a beautiful item of clothing; it makes you feel good about yourself. But while you can walk into a shop and choose a great outfit, you can't simply proffer a credit card and hey presto, you find yourself living in a dream home. Even money isn't necessarily a guarantee of a beautiful home; it takes time, effort and the knowledge required to get it right.

It is for all these reasons that when selling a property you shouldn't just focus on functional aspects of a development. Beautiful, well-chosen tableware, piles of beautiful tiles and bedlinen, books, flowers, accessories and pictures, all help to create an image of an attractive lifestyle. A deck with striking table and chairs might suggest easy Sunday mornings reading the papers. A rack that rattles with a few bottles of decent wine suggests a relaxed pace of life. Good quality, beautifully packed toiletries suggest a person of discernment and taste. Even if a potential purchaser doesn't recognise the fact, all these disparate elements combine to convince potential purchasers that this property won't just be a great place to live – it will completely change their lives. If it all sounds slightly nebulous – and even a little toe curling – that is because it is. But in the world of property development, if someone else is trying similar techniques, you have to as well.

All this might sound easy, but of course it's far from it. Few of us are born set dressers (and set dressing is what this is really all about) and the only option we have is to scour the pages of design magazines and books looking for ideas to slavishly copy. The secret is to create a feel that falls well short of looking contrived. Be prepared to try out lots of different ideas before you settle on one that works.

This mysterious art of 'styling' is rarely just about spending money – in fact there are times when it can save you money. Here's an example: you are developing a one bedroom property that might appeal to first time buyers. The flat has a wealth of attractive period detail that might be lost with a heavy-handed refurbishment. Instead, you go for a simple, arty look with painted white floors, a few well chosen items of vintage furniture, lots of pale fabrics and pale, chalky colours. What will sell this property is not deep pile carpets and fitted furniture but the promise of a simple, carefree lifestyle on a plate.

So what I'm suggesting here is *not* that you rush out just before a viewing and spend a fortune on fancy china, kitchen utensils, flowers, arty books and toiletries (it will only look contrived). But good flowers are the ideal last-minute buy (white being the safest colour). The point to be made here is that when you are furnishing a property it is best to focus on collecting together items that will create a pleasing feel. There's no point in investing huge sums of money in a property and then kitting it out with accessories that are inappropriate.

'Remember that the most beautiful things in the world are the most useless; peacocks and lilies, for instance.'

JOHN RUSKIN

Defining idea…

205

How did
it go?

Q   Now I'm really confused. I was under the impression that the best way to create a pleasing interior is to get rid of extraneous clutter but you seem to be advocating filling the space with knick-knacks.

A   *The idea of styling is not that you fill up space with knick-knacks – in fact, the decoration of a styled interior might be very spare. However, in a sparsely decorated spare interior, the items that are included will be very carefully chosen to project an image of a life lived beautifully.*

Q   If you don't mind me saying, isn't this a little ephemeral?

A   *Selling anything that must appeal to the senses can seem ephemeral.*

Q   You haven't mentioned scented candles anywhere, is this an oversight on your part?

A   *No, not really. Scented candles are now so ubiquitous that they may raise the suspicions of many punters. Often people assume that a scented candle is a means of hiding the smell of damp.*

47

From oven to table ...

A kitchen in which you can cook, eat and entertain suits modern life.

But in order to combine these two disparate functions, you need follow a few basic rules.

For many people, the dining room died a slow and unlamented death years ago. Derided by its critics as a cold, labour-intensive waste of space, in many homes it has been replaced by a large open-plan area that is an integral part of a kitchen. The space is achieved in a variety of ways; by extending to the side or rear of a property (in some cases in both directions) or by annexing adjacent rooms. However, the problem involves more than just finding the space; like any multifunctional room it requires careful planning if the results are not to be chaotic.

Because you will be creating one large open-plan space that will effectively have two different purposes you may want to find ways of creating two different zones that have subtly different styles. Zoning is a skill that is useful in the design of a variety of different rooms, particularly in the living room – a space that also has to incorporate a variety of different functions. In essence, it involves creating areas

Here's an idea for you... **If space is in short supply, you should consider fitting bench seats against one wall so that you can place the table tightly into a corner. While they aren't as convenient as chairs, bench seats do offer useful extra storage.**

that are loosely dedicated to different activities. The amount that you'll have to 'zone' an area will depend on how the kitchen is configured. For example, if a kitchen has a conservatory extension, there will be two distinct areas within the same space. When planning a kitchen diner, consider the following options for creating a distinct eating 'zone'.

THREE GREAT WAYS TO 'ZONE' A KITCHEN

1   *An island/peninsula unit.* This is one of the best ways to create a physical divide between the food preparation area of a kitchen and the eating and entertaining area. An island is a stand-alone unit at which food is prepared and equipment stored. The most sophisticated versions can include hobs, sinks and other appliances. As well as being a great way to 'zone' a kitchen it is also a very sociable place to cook, allowing you to talk to family and guests while you work. A peninsula unit is attached to the main run of kitchen cabinets, usually at a 90 degree angle. You may want to consider having a raised side that faces the dining area to shield the view of pots and pans. With careful planning you may also be able to incorporate a bar area at which simple meals can be eaten (it's the ideal place to feed breakfast to children when you are in a hurry).

2   *Decoration.* While you don't necessarily want to create a dramatic change between one space and another, a subtle change of paint colour is a great way to ring the changes. For example, if you are using one tone in the kitchen area, you could use a darker version in the other. Alternatively, consider wallpaper in the dining area and a complementary paint colour in the kitchen area.

You may also want to use lighting and accessories to create a slightly more glamorous mood in the kitchen area. A chandelier over the table will come into its own when you are entertaining. Also ensure that you have lots of versatile lighting options that will allow you to dim the lights in the kitchen – using subtle 'mood' lighting.

3   *Flooring*. Flooring is another discreet way to distinguish one area from another. If you use two dramatically different types of flooring there is a danger that the space will appear diminished. However, if you were to choose flooring in two different textures but similar colours (i.e. slate in the eating area and linoleum in the kitchen area) you would be creating an almost subliminal distinction between the two areas. Alternatively, you may decide to choose the same floor but with a darker colour in one area, and a lighter in another.

STORAGE

The best way to avoid chaos in a kitchen/dining room is to make sure you plan the storage amid the space in tandem. Try to dedicate storage to all the different functions of a room. The best way to do this is with either a dresser, a cupboard or a low storage unit that will accommodate the items – cutlery, table mats, accessories, napkins, tablecloths for instance. Inevitably a dining table will be used for far more than just eating and entertaining, so it makes sense to dedicate space to all the other activities that happen in the space. If you work at the table it might be a good place to keep a laptop or printer – and in family homes it is the ideal location for drawing and craft materials.

'Nothing would be more tiresome than eating and drinking if God had not made them a pleasure as well as a necessity.'

VOLTAIRE

Defining idea...

How did it go?

Q   **Won't having an island or peninsula unit in the middle of my kitchen get in the way and clutter up the space?**

A   *If you plan the space properly, this shouldn't be a problem. Also remember that a well-designed island will save you a huge amount of space elsewhere.*

Q   **A chandelier would look ridiculous in the kitchen that I'm planning; do you have any better suggestions?**

A   *Yes, a great option for hanging over kitchen tables is a row of three glass or aluminium shades.*

Q   **What about cabinetry? Shouldn't that blend with the eating area?**

A   *Yes it should – colours should complement one another. However, let the dining area follow the kitchen rather than the other way round. It is important that you choose the kitchen cabinets you want and make the dining area work with it.*

48

Drawing conclusions

Curtains, blinds and shutters are some of the trickiest elements in any decorating scheme.

But if you get it right, buyers won't just be impressed — they'll be trying to buy them from you.

A pair of curtains can make or break a room. It might be the pattern or colour – or it might be something more subtle, such as the texture, or the poles that they hang on. The problem is that taste is a very subjective area – particularly when it comes to curtains, so before investing any money it pays to do your research.

The other problem is that there are plenty of opportunities to get it wrong – there are, quite literally thousands of different patterns, colours and subtly different textures to choose from. And that's before you've chosen from one of the endless styles and accessories on offer. Or would you rather have blinds – or both? Or would shutters be the best option? With window treatments there are an almost infinite number of answers to any question.

CROWD PLEASING CURTAIN TREATMENTS

Because there is so much choice, it makes sense to focus on those styles and fabrics that are most likely to have maximum appeal.

1   *Curtains.* The ultimate option for both classic and contemporary interiors are heavy, interlined curtains made from a plain linen. Interlining – a thick layer of fabric that hangs between the fabric that faces the interior of a room and the outer lining that faces the window – will ensure that curtains offer excellent insulation against light, heat and cold. For classic interiors choose simple, painted or hardwood poles with a minimal amount of decorative detailing. For contemporary schemes opt for stainless steel or large 'rivet' headings that allow you to thread the curtain on to a pole.

2   *Blinds.* When choosing blinds, there's no doubt that handmade is best. There are a huge number of styles to choose from; but without a doubt the most versatile is a simple Roman blind that folds upwards to create a neat stack at the top of the window frame.

3   *Shutters.* Creating period-style shutters is a ruinously expensive process. However, 'plantation' shutters made from louvred panels offer a less expensive alternative – albeit it with a distinctly different look. Their adjustable blades can be angled so that that they allow light into a room while maintaining privacy. However, while they're cheaper than traditional shutters they are, nevertheless, significantly more expensive than either curtains or blinds.

Here's an idea for you... **If you can't decide between curtains and blinds you can easily mock them up with fabric. A crude gather can be made with a stapler and the curtains hung with masking tape. Mock up blinds in a similar way by hanging a panel of fabric in the window.**

CURTAINS VERSUS BLINDS

While they fulfil similar functions, curtains and blinds do have their own set of pros and cons. There's no doubt that curtains offer much better insulation against heat, light and cold than blinds. However, blinds create a much sleeker, more pared down look that make them ideal for contemporary interiors. They also require much less fabric. The ideal solution is a combination of the two – but this is expensive.

CURTAIN AND BLIND COLOURS

When considering a future sale, there's no doubt that plain, muted fabrics are a much safer option than patterned. Consider a textured fabric such as linen in creams, stones and browns – all are equally well suited to classic and contemporary interiors. Whichever colour you choose, ensure that it works with the other elements in the scheme such the wall colour, flooring and upholstery.

CHEAPER OPTIONS

There's no doubt that well-made curtains and blinds are expensive. When choosing window treatments for low value properties consider ready-made curtains. Another option is second-hand; although while they can seem like a good idea in principle, they rarely look as good as new and are rarely in a fabric that you want. Also remember that because they rarely fit perfectly, you may have to spend money on having them altered.

'At night, when the curtains are drawn and the fire flickers, my books attain a collective dignity.'
E M FORSTER

Defining idea…

SELLING WINDOW TREATMENTS ON

If you've invested in beautifully made window treatments, you might be able to re-coup some – or all – of the cost when you come to sell. Remember that many buyers may not have the time or the money to invest in curtain treatments, so they may be happy to pay over the odds. However, the chances are that it won't be practical to use them again, so even if you only sell them for a proportion of the cost, it is worth getting some money for them.

How did it go?

Q   While I want to create a contemporary look, I really want curtains because I need insulation from traffic noise. Won't curtains look out of place?

A   *If they are in the right fabric (i.e. a textured plain cloth such as linen) and you use the right type of curtain heading (i.e. rivets), then curtains look great in a contemporary scheme. Also remember that in a contemporary scheme blinds can almost seem too clinical. You don't want the room to look like a dentist's reception room.*

Q   Is pattern out of bounds?

A   *This is one of those areas where you have to be pragmatic. Pattern is a very subjective area, so it makes sense to go for plain fabrics that offer a combination of beautiful colour and texture. That way, they'll not only create a room that has more universal appeal but you are also more likely to be able to sell them on.*

49

In the mood

The secret of a successful decorating scheme is a tightly edited selection of fabrics, wallpaper and paint samples that will create exactly the look you want.

Yes, it's time to polish up your collage skills.

In the offices of interior designers you'll see collections of samples known as 'mood boards'. To the untrained eye these mysterious collections of samples look almost like pieces of conceptual art. But to designers and their clients they are the focus of all their attention. They are the tools that help them to ensure that colours, patterns and textures all work together in one harmonious scheme.

A mood board can be as simple or as elaborate as you like. At their most basic, mood boards can simply consist of a few fabrics and wallpapers stuck to a notice board or a piece of card. At their most elaborate, they can consist of painstakingly crafted collections, not just of fabrics, wallpapers and flooring but also photographs of items of furniture and lighting included in the scheme. The samples don't have to be large – just enough to give you a good idea of the colour and texture. It is best if the paint samples are applied to pieces of card.

Here's an idea for you...

The best way to learn about which colours and patterns work best together is to look at successful schemes and try to analyse why they work. You'll soon see patterns and formulas emerging that you'll be able to use as the basis for your own schemes.

The starting point of a mood board is to assemble all the different samples that you might be considering. It is best to choose them from as wide a range as possible, so try to build up a library of samples (it is important that each of these is marked with the manufacturer's or retailer's code). It also helps to have a few photographs of rooms that you like, which will help guide your initial choices. When comparing all these disparate elements side-by-side, it will soon become obvious which patterns and colours work well together and you'll be surprised at how quickly you'll come up with a cohesive scheme. The process doesn't have to be immediate; sometimes it will take place over a period of weeks. It is also helpful to mix in pictures of items of furniture, lighting and any pictures that you might be considering. If there are to be new purchases, use images from brochures or downloaded from the internet. If they are existing pieces, use photographs that you have shot against a plain background.

The most successful schemes are the result of a rigorous 'editing' process in which you start with a wide range of different ingredients and gradually hone them down to just a small handful. While all this might seem a little painstaking, there's no doubt that a mood board is an essential tool in making major decisions – and it will also mean that there are unlikely to be any nasty surprises when the scheme is completed. If you are decorating a number of rooms at the same time, it helps to work on the mood boards side-by-side, so that you will have a picture of how a sequence of rooms will appear.

CREATING A SAMPLES LIBRARY

If you are decorating a number of rooms, it makes sense to build up a collection of samples. Keep these in box files, divided into categories. The following checklist of categories should provide you with a good cross section of styles.

- Fabrics
  - plain neutrals
  - coloured plains
  - large checks
  - small checks
  - stripes
  - large florals
  - small florals
  - large graphics
  - small graphics
- Wallpapers
  - plains
  - stripes
  - large florals
  - small florals
  - large graphics
  - small graphics

'White ... is not a mere absence of colour; it is a shining and affirmative thing, as fierce as red, as definite as black ... God paints in many colours; but He never paints so gorgeously, I had almost said gaudily, as when He paints in white.'

G K CHESTERTON

Defining idea...

- Flooring
  - neutral carpet
  - coloured carpet
  - lino
  - vinyl
  - laminate
  - ceramic tiles
  - slate
  - limestone
  - stone paving
  - painted wood (make these samples up yourself)
- Tiles
  - basic tiles
  - mosaic tiles
  - textured tiles
- Paints
  - A core range of paint colours should be applied to pieces of card and should include the following: whites, off-whites, naturals, aquas, pale greens, deep aubergines, browns and reds.

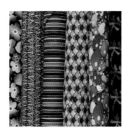

Q   **The aspect of creating a mood board that I find the most chal-   How did**
lenging is incorporating even the simplest pattern. Any tips?   it go?

A   *Pattern is a tricky area when developing a property, mainly because it is so*
subjective. That said, a simple graphic pattern can completely transform a
scheme (particularly in a dull room). The safest approach is to use just one
pattern on one of the elements in a scheme, i.e. the curtains, upholstery or
cushions and to 'anchor' it to the scheme by using a matching plain in the
same colour somewhere else in the room.

Q   **Is it safer to just use plains?**

A   *Yes, it is. But go for beautiful colours with texture such as linens or che-*
nilles. Or opt for very discreet pattern such as simple stripes or checks.
Alternatively, you could create a plain, muted backdrop and inject splashes
of muted colour and pattern.

Q   **Another ingredient in a scheme that gives me the fear is bright**
and dark colours. What do you advise?

A   *Any room will look larger and lighter if you use pale fabrics and paint.*
However, in a small room that has very little light it is sometimes better to
paint them in a dark colour that will effectively fudge the issue (it is a good
option for home offices and media rooms). Dark colours also have obvious
advantages on upholstery. You are right to be wary of bright colours in a
development; limit it to cushions and throws.

50

Up the wall

The treatment that you choose for the walls is an essential element in a scheme.

So it is important that they are a balanced part of the complete look, rather than the main attraction.

When you walk into an empty room, one of the first things that you look at is the walls. Yet when a room is full of furniture, window treatments and flooring, the walls often pale into insignificance. It is for this reason that when deciding how best to approach the walls, it is essential that you look at them within the context of every other element. Because of this, you should never make any major decisions about wall treatments without having first created a 'mood board' of the fabrics, flooring and furniture that you will be using in the scheme.

Mood boards are simple to create; just gather together samples of the materials that you are considering and you'll get a good idea of how their colours, textures and styles will work together. You can make a more elaborate mood board by assembling the samples of a board along with photographs of items of furniture

Here's an idea for you... **Allow yourself plenty of time to decide which curtain treatment works best in a room. Paint large areas of wall with samples and apply wallpaper to see how it looks and also how it reacts to the changing light during the course of a day.**

that will be in the room (either use images from brochures or, in the case of furniture that you already own, use your own photographs). Always remember to mark samples with details of the name, manufacturer and price.

Here are the pros and cons of the six main options for what you put on your walls.

- Paint
  Pros: This is the cheapest of all the options – particularly if you do the job yourself. It also offers the greatest range of colours, and it's relatively easy to maintain – just ensure that you keep a good supply of spare paint for chips and marks.
  Cons: It doesn't offer much in the way of depth or texture – although this can be achieved with specialist paint finishes.
- Wallpaper
  Pros: Hanging a good quality paper can make a room feel beautifully furnished – and if it's patterned you don't need to add any embellishment in the form of pictures or paintings. It is also far more robust than paint, and it's a very easy way to create striking impact. A large, graphic pattern offers a good half-way house between a traditional, decorative look and a minimal scheme. However, beware of small scale patterns that can look too busy. Alternatively, plain textured wallpapers – or designs with discreet pattern – offer a great way to add depth. For a contemporary look, consider having wallpaper on just one wall and a complementary colour on the other walls.

Cons: It's time consuming and fiddly to hang – and it's expensive to get some-one else to do it for you. While it is more robust than paint it is also more dif-ficult to repair. Also remember that if you want to create a house with universal appeal, there's no doubt that wallpaper is definitely an acquired taste.

- Tiles
  Pros: They are a functional and attractive option for bathrooms and WCs, allow-ing you to add colour, texture and a luxurious touch.
  Cons: They are fiddly and expensive to buy and hang – although in some cases, perhaps not as expensive as you think. Avoid patterned tiles at all costs – like any other patterned decorative feature, they are an acquired taste.

- Panelling
  Pros: A great way to create a cosy, intimate feel in a room and also to manipu-late its proportions (you can use its vertical and horizontal lines to trick the eye). It is also a great way of covering up wobbly walls. If you can't afford the real thing – and let's face it, who can? – you can create a similar feel with tongue and groove boards or MDF.
  Cons: Even if you do it cheaply, it is still more expensive than either paint or wallpaper.

- Fabric walling
  Pros: A great way to create a cosy, luxuri-ous feel.
  Cons: Extremely expensive – both in terms of materials and hanging.

'My wallpaper and I are fighting a duel to the death. One or other of us has to go.'
OSCAR WILDE

Defining idea...

How did it go?

Q   You seem have reservations about wallpaper, describing it as an 'acquired taste'. Is that a polite way of saying 'avoid like the plague'?

A   *No, not at all. While there are some wallpapers that have a very distinctive look, there are some types that will have universal appeal. There is no doubt that wallpaper creates a wonderful, intimate feel and there are plenty that will appeal to both hardened modernists and dyed-in-the-wool traditionalists. While it pays to be conservative when choosing wallpaper, you should also avoid using paints that will create a sea of blandness.*

Q   I'm not sure how I could use panelling to 'manipulate proportions'. Could you elaborate please?

A   *Let me give you an example. If a ceiling is very high, you can create a slightly more intimate feel by splitting the wall space laterally with panelling. It never helps to have too much vertical space in a room and panelling is a good way to break it up.*

Q   You haven't mentioned mirror – isn't that a good wall treatment?

A   *It is, but only in small quantities – and in quite extreme situations. If a room is very dark you might decide to cover one wall in mirror to maximise any natural light – however, if you cover more than just one wall in mirror you run the risk of creating a space that feels like a fairground attraction.*

51

It's not all about you

When developing a house with a view to a sale, it's important that you regard potential buyers as customers.

And in this game, as in so many, the customer is king.

There is sense in which property development is a service industry. If you want to maximise the value of a house, your own tastes and needs really have very little to do with it. Good developers regularly make aesthetic and financial decisions that they would never make if they were designing a house purely to suit their own needs. More often than not, they spend money on things that they wouldn't dream of treating themselves to – and similarly, they will often economise on things that they wouldn't dream of stinting on in their own homes. But then this is business – and to be successful in business you have to make hard-nosed financial decisions.

Also remember that a well-developed property is more than just bricks and mortar. The best are those that offer a beautiful environment that is, in effect, 'off the shelf'. They will offer a look that most people, particularly those with busy lives and families would never have the time or skill set to be able to create on their own. When

Here's an idea for you...

It helps to write a list of all the features that you think are essential to maximise the value of a property and your own wish list. The chances are that there might be much more overlap than you think. When reviewing your own list think long and hard about those that you can do without.

fashion designers create an item of clothing that will sell in its thousands, they make one with universal appeal rather than something that will suit them.

Overriding your financial and aesthetic sensibilities requires a great deal of will power – but once you have assumed the mindset, it will be plain sailing. Even if you are refurbishing a house that you won't be selling for another five years, it will help you think about it on two very different levels; as a development opportunity – and also, naturally, as your own home. The chances are that the two might be very different. If you really find it impossible to live in an environment without impressing your personality on it, then try and limit your personal touches to things that can be removed or replaced ahead of a sale.

The secret to identifying the development opportunity is to work out the target market of a property – and the best way to do that is decide who which type of buyers are most likely to pay the most for it. To focus your mind, it is best not to think of them as 'potential purchasers' but customers.

Let's take the hypothetical example of a ground floor two bedroom flat in a converted Georgian building that has a small garden and close the centre of an affluent provincial town. There are two ideal customers for the property. The first is a
well-heeled young professional who wants to be close to rail links and the town's
nightlife. The other is a cash-rich elderly couple who are selling their large house
in a nearby village who don't want to be reliant on a car. Then there's a third set
of needs in this equation – yours. Let's say in this hypothetical scenario, you are a
middle-aged divorced Francophile horticulturist with two children who come to
stay at weekends.

They key is to create a property that will cater for all these disparate needs – with
the result that you should resist the temptation to create a high maintenance
garden, an elaborate Chateau-style 'salon' and a second bedroom that is based on
the set of Harry Potter. Equally, however sensible it might sound to fit support
rails in the bathroom for the hypothetical elderly couple, they might give the
wrong message to the young internet entrepreneur who is another of your target
customers.

The secret to a successful development is to sublimate your own tastes and needs
and focus purely on creating an environment that will appeal to affluent buyers,
both young and old. The answer is likely to be
good quality detailing, cool colours, a simple
painted kitchen and a good quality bathroom   *'Objectivity requires taking*   Defining
(but probably not with a hot tub) and a low   *subjectivity into account.'*   idea...
maintenance garden with a deck or terrace.   LORRAINE CODE

How did it go? **Q I find the idea of living surrounded by plain neutral paint and fabric, completely abhorrent. Is individuality really such a turn off for potential buyers? I have been told that I have quite good taste.**

A   *You might have quite good taste in some people's eyes but it is a very, very subjective area. The chances of finding a buyer who will share exactly the same aesthetic sensibilities as you is a long shot. Also, the reality might not be nearly as bad as it sounds. You have to realise that if you want to max-imise the value of a property you need to make decisions that make good business sense rather than anything that is based on personal whim.*

Q Could I create an environment of my own choice and then re-decorate when the time comes to sell?

A   *You could – but unless you are taking a long-term view it is quite an expen-sive option. Also, remember that it isn't just about the decoration of a property; it's also about the way that you organise space – and large scale projects such as fitting bathrooms and kitchens are hugely costly to change.*

Sell, sell, sell

There are plenty of myths about tricks that will help to sell property – but most of them will set alarm bells ringing.

After all, it's the house that you're selling not your cooking skills or taste in music.

Filling a property with the smell of frying onions, freshly baked bread or just-brewed coffee are just some of the tricks that are supposed to work wonders on potential buyers. Not only are these techniques unproven but the chances are that they'll give the impression that you're trying to mask the smell of something suspicious. It is hard to pull the wool over the eyes of potential buyers (and well nigh impossible to try to con a surveyor); the best policy is either to sort them out or be honest about them. If you do have a problem with damp or drains the chances are that they'll raise their ugly heads at some stage.

Here is a list of tips on creating the ideal scenario for a sale ...

1   *Clean obsessively*. It is hard to stress how important this is. In advance of a viewing you should thoroughly clean a house so that it shows few signs of life. In addition to some 'long term' cleaning jobs such as windows, upholstery and

curtains – and obvious areas to focus on such as kitchens and bathrooms – pay particular attention to light switches, door plates and door mats. Also a bed always looks better when it is made up in freshly laundered linen. It is also worth taking a similar approach to bathroom towels and dish cloths (you may want to keep unused spares specifically for viewings). The advantage of cleanliness isn't about appearances – a room will also smell clean, too. The smell of a newly washed kitchen floor is infinitely more enticing than the smell of freshly baked bread!

Here's an idea for you...

It's worth having a trial run of your preparation routine so that you can pre-empt any potential problems well in advance of a viewing. Carry out the suggestions on the list of ideas above and see what improvements you could make; in particular, how furniture is arranged – this can have a huge impact on the way that a room looks. You should also divide a plan for last minute storage of items that you might want to hide away.

2   *Air rooms*. This might sound obvious but like cleaning, it is completely essential. A couple of hours before a viewing will take place, open all the windows and doors in a property, even if it is in the depths of winter, and then allow enough time to allow the temperature to reach your preferred levels.

3 *Remove all signs of life.* Removing clothing and personal possessions isn't just about looks – it also helps to create an anonymous feel, similar to that in a hotel room. Also remove anything to do with personal grooming such as razors and toothbrushes. Be sure to dry baths, showers and bathroom floors thoroughly after use. Anything that suggests that you have recently been there are also a no no – i.e. smouldering fires.

4 *Mow lawns.* It is essential that all lawns are immaculate, even in the winter. Newly-mown lawns look and smell extremely appealing.

5 *Be out.* No potential buyer likes the owner to be lurking around in the background; it makes them feel awkward. And let's be honest, they might not like the look of you. It's far better that you are nothing but a figment of their imagination.

6 *Flower power.* While they might deny it, few people fail to be moved by the sight of a few well placed vases of flowers. Don't bother with arrangements or go over the top; simple bunches of unmixed white or pink flowers such as roses, peonies and tulips are all that are required.

A CARDINAL SIN

While there is nothing wrong with using scented candles or air fresheners for your own personal use, never under any circumstances use them before a viewing. As well as raising suspicion, your olfactory system can be enormously picky about what it does and doesn't like.

> **'The worst enemy of creativity is self doubt.'**
> SYLVIA PLATH

Defining idea...

How did
it go?

**Q   Surely I'd be a better at selling my property than an estate
agent?**

A   *You wouldn't be better than a good estate agent. If you don't have confi-
dence in the agent who'll be doing the viewings, then change agent – or
specify the person who you want to sell the property. It's all about spe-
cialisation of labour. You'd be unlikely to try to fix your own central heating
boiler, so why do think that you'd be any better at selling your property?*

Q   What is the best way to brief an estate agent?

A   *It is important that you brief everybody who will be doing viewings – try to
insist on this. Alternatively, write a briefing document in bullet-point form.
You should create a short list of the benefits that you want to highlight
from the position to any internal feature that you feel sets the property
apart from the herd.*

**Q   I can't believe that a few bunches of flowers are going to sell a
property that has had a considerable amount of time and money
invested in it.**

A   *The attraction of small touches such as flowers is almost subliminal. They
might not register immediately but they'll be part of an overall impression.
Also, if you need evidence of the power of the flower, just look at pictures
of the interior of beautiful house, hotels and restaurants. The common
denominator? Yes, plenty of flowers.*

The end...

Or is it a new beginning?

We hope that the ideas in this book will have inspired you to look at your home through the eyes of potential buyers. You should now be armed with insider tips and exciting ideas for maximising the value of your home. Maybe we've even helped you change a difficult-to-sell property into one that has the local estate agents salivating..

So why not let us know all about it? Tell us how you got on. What did it for you – what really added thousands onto the value of your house? Maybe you've got some tips of your own you want to share (see next page if so). And if you liked this book you may find we have even more brilliant ideas that could change other areas of your life for the better.

You'll find the Infinite Ideas crew waiting for you online at www.infideas.com.

Or if you prefer to write, then send your letters to:
Decorate to speculate
The Infinite Ideas Company Ltd
36 St Giles, Oxford, OX1 3LD, United Kingdom

We want to know what you think, because we're all working on making our lives better too. Give us your feedback and you could win a copy of another *52 Brilliant Ideas* book of your choice. Or maybe get a crack at writing your own.

Good luck. Be brilliant.

Offer one

CASH IN YOUR IDEAS

We hope you enjoy this book. We hope it inspires, amuses, educates and entertains you. But we don't assume that you're a novice, or that this is the first book that you've bought on the subject. You've got ideas of your own. Maybe our author has missed an idea that you use successfully. If so, why not put it in an email and send it to: yourauthormissedatrick@infideas.com, and if we like it we'll post it on our bulletin board. Better still, if your idea makes it into print we'll send you four books of your choice. or the cash equivalent. You'll be fully credited so that everyone knows you've had another Brilliant Idea.

Offer two

HOW COULD YOU REFUSE?

Amazing discounts on bulk quantities of Infinite Ideas books are available to corporations, professional associations and other organisations.

For details call us on:
+44 (0)1865 514888
fax: +44 (0)1865 514777
or e-mail: info@infideas.com

Where it's at ...

brilliantideas   **Start changing your life in five minutes...**

With the **52 Brilliant Ideas** series you can enhance your existing skills or knowledge with negligible investment of time or money and can substantially improve your performance or know-how of a subject over the course of a year. Or day. Or month. The choice is yours. With the help of our expert authors you can achieve your goals and live your life on your own terms – remember, one brilliant idea can change your life.

Visit our website at **www.infideas.com** to see all of our inspirational titles.

Join our mailing list at **www.infideas.com** and be entered into our monthly prize draw to win 3 books of your choice from our bestselling **52 Brilliant Ideas** series worth over £35. In addition, the first 20 readers to email decorate@infideas.com with their name, address and telephone number will win a copy of one of our top humour titles, *Getting away with it: Short cuts to the things you don't really deserve.*

Start changing your life in five minutes... with the **52 Brilliant Ideas** series.